THE BRITTLE FOUNDATIONS OF OUR CIVILIZATION

A book by Paul James Gabol

THE BRITTLE FOUNDATIONS OF OUR CIVILIZATION

Foundation:

"In engineering, a base upon which something is supported. By analogy, in Social Science, a basis or principle, even an undisputed axiom" (from the 'Just to Be Clear' Dictionary)

Civilization:

"Culture or society. The assembly of characteristics of common life within a human group at a given place or time" (from the above mentioned Dictionary, as well)

FOREWORD

Let's follow

We are followers. By nature we follow. Follow what others do, repeat what others say. Our words are echoes of others. After all, we're only animals that must obey a code deeply embedded in our genes to be a group, to concur and to follow. There are of course those that become the leaders, the alpha individuals that set, from time to time, the new path or that reinforce the old one. But, even those guiding the rest of us, do it within certain boundaries, applying specific rules created before their time, struggling to make changes, to improve our lives and of course to shift the behavior of the followers. Let them worry, let us follow.

Our civilization comes in a package that tells us what to do in every aspect of our lives, how we are born and how we die. We are told what to eat and what not. How to dress, when to study and when to work. We are organized. Every one of us has a place in the huge organism we call our society. We learn what's good and what is not. We become guardians of our beliefs, we follow.

The pinnacle of civilizations?

Needless to say that our civilization is the best there is, otherwise we would not have it that way. We are the first world, the "world class" and our truth… well our truth knows no frontiers. Yes, we are the expanding Western Civilization.

We have used any tools available throughout time to impose our way of life. We have conquered. We have marketed our ideas and our products. We are globalizing our core values, our moral beliefs. Is it rather pandemic?

Our standards are setting the free everything: free market, freedom of thought and speech, free enterprise and free choice. The same standards are achieving justice for everyone, democracy, equality, there is nothing but a bright future ahead. For some reason, however, the past and present tell other story: they are somber, something is wrong.

Our morals contradict our deeds

We are continuously contradictory. Facts and words do not match. Sometimes we see it, raise an eyebrow, scratch our head and decide everything is too complex to fully understand it. Most of the time we develop systems and subsystems thickly layered to model cause and effect, theories to understand what is happening socially and economically, but fail to explain the odd unexpected results. We are unable to predict our society's future with accuracy, or even show logic on its actual behavior. The underlying reason is that our civilization is founded with brittle materials, because for some it is convenient, immoral but convenient. Some, not we, yet, we go along.

Where are we?

I had the strangest dream last night -don't we all?-. We were walking the aisles of an airport dimly, indirectly lit, yet bright enough to see every detail. A soothing bluish light. Perfect white tile floors and also white blue-lined columns, straight where the corridors were a long endless line, yet curved, arched where the corridors circled. The place was almost empty, but no question it was an airport.

"Where are we?" someone asked. Is it…? No, looking at the architecture it couldn't be… For certain it was the first world. But coming to think of it, there are first world airports in lower level countries.

"We didn't crash, right?" somebody else said and then it dawned. Our plane had made an emergency landing in another West-Civ. country. I recognized the flag and its logo. That place where I had promised myself not to set a foot on, because only two generations ago my family had given blood fighting this fierce enemy that today is our ally and above all our trade partner. Shockingly our partner. What about our core values? Trade over dignity, makes you wonder.

The picture reeled in and all started again, but different, improved. We descended at will from the plane, uncontrolled, no customs, no need for a correct colored passport, free to move about. A group of multinational strangers bound by fate, equals in almost every way, leaping into a world seeming to lack regulations. No beggars around the corner as it often happens in my home town. No stained walls or littered floors. No billboards on competing products. Strange, not our world. Even the flag faded away. No more emblem. Only the soft colors and a faint violin melody. Where are we? Everything suddenly so perfect that it couldn't be our world. Well, it wasn't.

A trait, a foundation?

The features of our civilization may not be so difficult to see, they are however tangled in a continuum where the beginning of one is the end of another, which in turn is pasted to yet another one. It becomes truly puzzling to find what came first, what second. What gave birth to which. What is just a trait on the outside and what else is a true foundation, a true core value that rules our lives at the most private of our moments. What determines our goals and thus the developments of our science, our modernity and, needless to say, our philosophy. Same goes for the laws we place alongside of the natural ones and the effort we make to enforce them because they are not natural, then hard to follow. Maybe it is not that important to find out which ones we should look closely at. Let's look at them all, the outstanding ones, and find the common ground to them. If that common ground is not to our taste, well let's find a solution. If it is agreeable let's enjoy it and stop wondering about our present and future. I invite you to place the boat in cruise control and steer it through the deep waters of our civilization: our foundations.

PART I
FOUNDATIONS

PART I
FOUNDATIONS

ONE- Snob

Snob:

"Someone who admires or holds extreme respect for higher social positions or social superiors, thus feeling inferior; despises its own kind and those below; and strives to associate and become as those admired" (from the 'Don't You Feel Excluded' Dictionary)

We are all snobs. According to the above definition practically all of the individuals in our society are snobs. Have you ever asked for an autograph? Is your favorite player's picture stapled, or even better, framed on your wall? Is there a picture in your office or living room with you next to a prominent politician? Do you follow the lives of the famous on the social media? Do you treat with outmost respect those whose names are anteceded by a title? Do you proudly show the brand of your sweatshirt? If yes, you are a snob and yes you are a true West-Civ. bred person.

Let's see how our society works. We are followers I said, as there are leaders. In our society the leader, whether or not morally and factually a true leader, uses a title that will distinguish her or himself -the new equality trait of our culture- from the rest. Precisely from-the-rest. There is of course a self-infatuation in doing this, but also, certainly, it helps to reaffirm the position and bring authority to it.

There are degrees to this. As a part of nature, we behave alike but not exactly the same as our neighbor. We can be modeled within the statistical domain and there will be a Gauss bell where we can be pinpointed. We will belong to a certain area of that standard normal distribution. We can either be the ones on the extreme sides or the ones at the center. The shape of the bell, as it comes to the snobbish behavior, could change from country to country or from region to region, so as to acquire that of the Eiffel Tower or that of a turtle's carapace. Nevertheless the trend remains, Snob it is.

Titles are everywhere. From ancient times, royalty and nobility, from the king to the simple gentlemen, the omnipresent military with all its ranks. Then nowadays, the newer forms of government, all with its pyramidal structure, give us an accurate sense of hierarchy for the power bodies in the life of mankind. But, what about titles for common people? Is there anything left for us? Anything to reach at? Yes there is: plenty of enterprises and organizations; available posts for presidents, directors, managers and its vice or sub positions, a title to get a hold on. In other grounds, more of it is offered now as diplomas and certificates for minors, majors and post-graduate studies. We find a reason for pride and we set our targets and achieve our objectives. The only catch is that it seems that our goals are to get those titles, not the qualification, abilities and knowledge that come with the undertaken studies. Sure we will find a job -hopefully related to our credentials- and, today, must certainly with a better chance to compete with others for that position, moreover if those others do not have the qualification proof, regardless of their de facto preparation.

The papers attained have also degrees of validity. Which school, board, organization or even which country is saying you are qualified? There are A+ institutions and, well of course C- ones. Where did you say you graduated? Those institutions then in turn get graded by third parties under qualifications systems introduced by the most powerful and highly recognized organizations in the field. It is a never ending ladder.

If this is true for education, why not do the same for the companies? Why not, in order to gain an advantage over the competition, we bring into the picture a trade permit. Let us not call it a permit, rather a qualification system for process quality, for safety, for environmental protection, because, how can I trust your product if there are injuries in your freight yard, for instance? Can I? I will tell you how to do it. I will certify you as reliable. It will take an effort, but when you reach that point you will be very satisfied and able to trade. Did I mention that upgrades will be a winding road constant? O yes, continuous improvement. Again I will monitor your achievements and certify your status. Think of all the titles you will be able to hang on your meeting rooms, your reception halls and your CEO's office. Well, if you want, it can be in your CFO's one.

To make it even better, imagine that you can make a crisscrossing certification, the ultimate proof of performance. You comply with it all. You have a name. You possess the power to dictate trends, to be a role model, to endorse ideas and support actions by merely saying so. Whether right or wrong you become the truth.

What about the untitled people, the ones with a trade such as a baker, a shoemaker, a blacksmith, a farmer, a mechanic, an electrician, a plumber, a carpenter, a mason or a gardener? What can they do? They have been as useful before and long after the title frenzy, but we the snobs do not think so. How about a plain steel, paper, textile or lumber mill worker? Their very valuable work is simply not recognized. It has always been tough, but is not getting any better for them. In our first world the title, not the actual job, is ahead in the pyramid.

In the end, we believe that it is for the better. In the end, we accept the requirements imposed on us. We run, chase the train and finally grab a railing and hop on it.

Of course we will throw out anything that will resemble a connection to the opposite side of success and we will dress accordingly: downtown-like, office-like. But before that we will get an education. It will be worth it...Wait a minute, will it?

Consider that the average tuition time for a college degree is around 4.5 years. The tuition and fees vary widely depending on the institution qualifications, the country, the citizenship and the course language. Usually favored are the residents taking courses in the native language. In some cases it can be a free taught degree, but it may turn out to be as far as 45,000 USD per year. If we place a fairly current sum of 20,000 USD per annum cost, we would be talking of a 90,000 USD degree cost. Maybe these figures are acceptable considering the amount you will get paid once you get a job, once in business. How long will your pay-back period be?

At exactly the same interval that individuals are preparing themselves to go into the labor market, companies are also spending money to prepare those who have already enrolled. Their spending averages 1,500 USD per employee per year, involving an annual 3 day per capita training effort. The latter implies that an individual with a degree spends as much as 30 times the amount of money and about a thousand fold of its time just to be able to work there, within the registered system. Why isn't your employer paying for your basic training? Who is making the effort and who profits from it? Who is taking advantage? Who invented and sustains this system that depletes the individual in favor of the corporation? Still, believe me, it is worth it.

In some cases tuition is covered by government expenditure, it turns out to be free for the individual but not for the society. If the job is to be performed within the public service, it seems to come about even. If conversely it's not, then the society as a whole is working for the enterprises, even if these promote jobs and pay taxes, turning-in some dividends unto our society. Just some, because that is dependent of the careful handling of accounting statements where gains must be presented as low as possible. The winner appears not to be the government nor the society.

The qualifying system feeds itself and overwhelms practically everything in our connected world today. On its own, it has created a new branch of jobs that inspect and certify, on a yearly basis, individuals, corporations and even governments. This jobs of course do not add value to the economy and decrease everybody's gain, starting at the bottom of the production chain. This is a matter to be reviewed later on.

The social need to belong, to be a part of something, goes beyond a title. As mentioned before, fame takes its own credit. Pro sports can deliver this unwritten powerful diplomas to a very limited number of people, leaving the rest, alas, with an unaccomplished dream. Fame can be also reached in the electronic field of the social media: self-made images can and are a very powerful tool to be somebody.

 Being certified, being licensed, permitted is a survival need. That tag imposed on us is also a control feature or, at least, it opens the door to certain degree of it. But we want to be noticed, don't we?

Long time ago, when I was very young and the internet had not yet interfered with the personal life, I had the unique opportunity to meet an ambassador from a small country – you know, those countries that, although part of our civilization, we as snobs look down upon for the simple reason of being small-, a country probably more successful than the others assembling the block of our civilization, but by no means the leader and not as powerful -not as threatened either-.

I had met the man in question while performing a job that related his Embassy with my employer needs to purchase technology from that country. That particular case was important to him and he believed also for his country, since it would develop a new line of business, a new trade with ours.

One day I was waiting for him at the embassy lobby for a meeting with a group of entrepreneurs also interested on the subject, when I was summoned to his office, because he had some comments on the agenda. As soon as I entered he called from the side of the chamber where a small lavatory stood.

"My apologies Paul," he said, "I have to do this twice a day, three times if I have evening meetings." He was shaving. "Which I have a lot. And which I enjoy, by the way"
"Hello Sir," I said.
"Get a seat. No, just better stand there. I have a change of strategy for the meeting," looking at me sideways through the mirror.
"What do you have in mind?"
"Nothing very different, but you see, there is someone called-up that I can't figure out, and I'm afraid –well...concerned- he will make the meeting go astray"
"Should we, after introductions, should you, should I, propose them to share their view point first?" And after a silent moment while he gave a last stroke he said,
"I'll do the talking, you give me your advice later. You know who I am talking about?" Yes I did.

I've never cared for a picture in the paper, smiling next or shaking hands with an important person. I've had some chances, here and there, to be close to, or even share a few words, with CEO's, highly influential people, a President even, but never an encounter with the person behind the *façade*. Only that time. Years after, I realized what an incredible person he was and how humble we could all be.

TWO- The hive

Hive:

"In Biology, a bee's nest or the colony itself. By analogy, something busy, active, buzzing and full; crowded" (from the 'Analogies of Life' Dictionary)

Who doesn't love the outdoors? A sunset on a secluded beach, a cascade on the mountains, the gentle flow of a creek or the roar of a magnificent white water river, the thick humid forest, a lake teeming with life, the snowy peaks or the breathtaking view of a desert are the many representations of the wild we say to love. Really?

The population trend has packed the human animal in something called cities. The largest the better. Skyscrapers and buildings holding office spaces and housing ones as well. The tallest the better. Thousands and thousands of inhabitants per square mile.

At the beginning, people lived in the countryside, where naturally occurring landscapes are the ones we delight to portrait on the wall of our 22nd story apartment downtown. A place where we hardly know the neighbors but that through a complex system of clothing codes, along with maybe gadgets in view, hair and skin color, and perfume brands, allows us to distinguish the beings that belong from those that should be elsewhere, in another nest, at the great hive. I wonder if there is a tiny tattoo on the forehead that only the alike are able to see, or a scentless pheromone, distinguishing us.

Our everyday life starts there at the crowded altitudes of the city and, after leaving our almost claustrophobic home, we descend a hopefully empty lift, to be thrown into a heavily occupied sidewalk and street, only to improve on a packed subway train, where voids exist only above our heads. Needless to say about the elevator at work or the cubicle H4 at the flat where we spend most of the day.

Lunch is also a communion with unknown people that, again, are alike somehow. The cafeteria we attend, every noon or afternoon, has the same parishioners and any stranger would be spotted instantly and at least, with subtle ways, ousted from the place beyond its surrounding invisible border. We may wait for a table to be freed and may be prompted to a quick meal amid a buzzing of cacophonic laughs, shouts and conversations. People, people everywhere, talking, smiling, frowning…communicating. People.

The way back home may be interrupted to meet another crowd at a bar, for a not so cheap beer, or at a coffee shop for a very expensive few ounces of brew. Who cares! How could we be bothered by the lines, the noise, the waiting, if we have in exchange the lack of room, the mates and the suffocating ambiance?

Is it melancholy that drives us to think that we actually love the wild? Out there no museums to be found, no theaters, no football fields, no malls. Malls above all, because the weekend without a people gathering would be an uneventful one, it would be empty and dull.

Day after day we have our chores. Regardless of its kind or hierarchy, we make a standard effort and deliver a standard result that we benchmark against other nests or hives. In the end…No, there is no end. We do this routine until the moment we cannot endure it. I don't know why we bother studying insects to match their behavior and produce the yet incipient artificial intelligence, if watching a turnpike full of slowly moving cars at dusk or people crossing at a street corner, would be enough for it: hive conducts self -explained.

Somewhere in time, depending on the country in our civilization, we were drawn to the cities and we expanded in them, populated them and invented a life we call productive.

It is not that we emptied the countryside, no. The countryside kept its share of people, but the city overgrew -though we're proud about it- oversized itself and gave its daughters and sons -that never knew there was a wild except for movies and snap-shots-, a place to live and work. Work that in some cases meant factory productions, but that in many resulted in office jobs enlarging the service industries and supposedly our GDP.

More than half a century ago, sci-fi promised us a better world, a place where humans would finally be able to rest. The hard work would be over and robots –in many cases humanoids- would perform the needed chores, from mining and farming to manufacturing. We would be at ease. Reality tell us now, that the more comfort we get, the easier tasks we have, it is all overturned into a maximized volume of work, it is converted into an equation about enhancing productivity. We have become busier animals in crowded spaces. The cows from the prairie are now being housed and milked in a stable. Yes, we roam as well.

Some others envisioned a sour future, where we would become a machine within a complex system of production and life. They preconized a world with indoors only, yes, without the outdoors, where we would remain from birth to death doing what we would be told, specialized in this or that for the greater good. Families would disappear. No more mom-dad-and-children. Our chosen descendants would only be known to the embryo farms, nursery workers and the conditioning system teachers–sorry, schooling system-, devoted to the care and upbringing of the new members of the society. Birth control would be a must and natural birth forbidden, as a need to preserve society's stability in number and desires, and a way to correctly assign adult tasks. We would be controlled, watched, directed and restrained, but extremely happy.

In a certain way, both ideas converge. They were quite right, except for the happiness and the fact that not all of us get the comfort, not all of us get the reward of the new modern city life. In an ironic exchange, we have also lost some of the essentials. Maybe not. Maybe it is just my narrow and romantic idea about human relationships.

Our life begins at a system approved hospital, where a bunch of crying babies are individually wrapped and bedded in large rooms, where they tend to remain quiet before being delivered home, though not for long, since they soon begin a steady programming –named education- through nursery, elementary school and so on, sharing their time with equals and away from the said-to-be family that gave them birth. We our bound to socialize on every day of our lives; be a part of something at school -art, sports-; belong to an ensemble; think as a whole; acquire group values, hopefully being sheltered by our classmates and upon agreement on thoughts, goals and dreams -slanted or biased, as some may think-. Later on, repeating the formula at work, while some are projected to higher instances. At the end of your life, if you are lucky, your family will take care of you or, if not, a different kind of nursery will wall your laughs and tears. All within the rules of the community.

Not surprisingly, there is very little spare time available. Even less if we belong to that commuter crowd that spends a sixth of its day traveling from house to work and back. But if we are lucky and have enough income to do something else than watch ball games on the TV, we will socialize at the trail, the gym, the sports court, the museum and the opera house, where we will have encounters and the most superficial relationships of our lives, but, who ever heard of ants or bees having a relationship longer than a rub on the way or a slight touch of antennae? The bee dance, you say? Yes, we do have ballrooms.

Let us go back to our cubicle H4 in the third level tunnel –at the skyscraper, our vertical nest-. I am puzzled. How does our activity in our precious hive produce food? How does it make ore extraction happen? How does it fish or manufacture clothing? Are we actually depending on –or in the worst sense, exploiting- a few out there? Do we even stop a moment to think if our jobs are really useful? Maybe the best answer to these is "I don't know, but it is what it is." Often I think of ourselves as blind parasites guided by our DNA code, living because we are alive, not knowing where we are, but being nourished by other people's effort, producing waste somebody else takes care of. We don't have a comprehensive view of the rest of the world and, in many cases, neither of our country. We take for granted what is being fed to us. That is our truth, the colony's principles: crowded, mechanical, absent-minded.

THREE- The fourth power - Freedom

Power:

"In Physics, work done over a period of time. In Social Sciences, the act or capacity to control people or events. Also: strength, command" (from the 'You Better Stay in Line' Dictionary)

Freedom:

"The right to think, speak, act and choose without coercion or limit" (from the 'Fictions of Life' Dictionary)

We don't have personal thoughts, they have been implanted. Every day there is a new insertion, some deletion and many reinforcements. We have our opinion designed. The written, televised or radial facts, statements or judgments come to us in the form of a continuous shower or at drenching intervals during the day. Our minds are shaped by the media. Our civilization requires a constant fortification and the press has self-given the right to be our spokesperson.

We do notice that, from time to time, the media supports a government, a move, a thought, a trend, then it shifts and becomes a harsh critic, even of the system where it stands. Sometimes it's condescending, sometimes aligned, some others defiant and seldomly heroic, but omnipresent.

Freedom of speech is a big asset. For many, it is the definition of our civilization, the iconic value, but there is a catch to it: we can only think and express what we know and have learned within the boundaries of our sub-world –please note that sub does not imply inferior, but only a distinctive segment of the whole set-. In any culture, the common view starts at the values and beliefs of the culture itself, it necessarily sees wrong in other cultures doing. Our fate is written: meals, religion, clothing, marriage, children upbringing, economy, in one word, everything. We are locked inside the walls of ourselves. We can't help it. Guess what, it is the same for the others, the different from us. Difficult task for world communication, hence, we will leave that one to the Armed Forces or, in the last resort, to the Diplomatic Service. In the best of settings on civilizations inter-contact, we are short of acting and thinking objectively, because we are ignorant of other peoples and cultures. In the worst position we just scorn them.

Ironically, change usually comes from abroad, Ideas we learned elsewhere -if it isn´t nature that slaps us, from time to time, to make us react-. We improve, we invent...we change. We compare ourselves to nature –as if we were equals to it in the universe-, we also test ourselves against others and then we change. Among us, there are only a few shift makers, but once they act, we are sure to follow, sooner or later.

Back to our problem. We are short sighted. Our myopia disables us from true freedom of speech. We repeat in several ways what it is in "our nature", what we were breastfed. Liberals of today become the conservatives of tomorrow. There are things and concepts we revise today and become the thought-dissidents. We act and become revolutionaries and, in the end, we run out of ideas, out of strength and we pause. We decide there is no more to be changed, no more to be improved. We become stagnant, just in time for the arrival of the new dissidents -our daughters and sons-, ready to sweep our establishment.

Once upon a time there were no social networks or at least not as we know them. When people had the time, they would gather at home with friends to discuss the array of problems in their community: the need for a doctor; the water reservoir leak; a corn plague; the lack of rain, the road repair; the coming of new settlers; the need of a new mill; and the lack of jobs. Someone was always in charge of the last decision and someone was always also in disagreement. From just a simple viewpoint to conspiracy plots, freedom of speech was exercised within the protecting walls of a home.

With time, private homes were not the only place to meet and disagree, a table at a pub or a café housed the discontent, who would whisper or, if extremely confident, brave or careless, shouted their belief to save their region or state, without nothing more than a relief outburst of mind - machinations would still be and will continue to be held private-. Public opinion would rise from beer mugs with the same inaccuracy of cause and effect between problems and solutions, as we encounter today. Of course, the impact of those small meetings and ideas would be very small, since travelling on horseback or at the speed of a swollen sail, could find the answer in a dead or overturned governor, before the news or abdication ideas arrived distorted for the desired change.

Later on, the telegraph and telephone added speed and certainty to the ideas, while, at the same time, venturing some of the system shifters out of the homes and unto the public tables. Telephone became specially precious and reliable to convey ideas and freedom of speech, but every move and invention always meets its countermeasure: taps in this case. End of conversation.

In our times, ideas and information have exploded. We can talk, text, write, film, record anything that comes to our minds, within seconds, somebody else can assess the validity and power of our thoughts. Come to think about it...not quite. It is true that we can say anything we want and post it any way we want, however it isn't correct to believe we can suitably judge it, first because we hear too many things about an enormous amount of subjects, making us unable to grasp all of it and, secondly, because we are ignorant.

Freedom of speech in this sense is very dangerous. We can slander at ease. We can lie just as comfortably. We can be mistaken without remorse or consequence, because we are free to do so. Imagine now those who carry a laptop backpack, a badge, glasses to look clever or secretly tape a "chance" meeting, instead of the most common cell phone recording or the more openly camera videotaping. Picture those that call themselves "The Press" –as from pressure- now making the same solid statements to be carried to all people - the least favored included-, to make it stick as the truth of the moment. Again, our lack of knowledge steals from us the possibility to recognize the veracity of the said things. Pounding the statement, once and again, we come to believe in it, we relay it and boost its value. Understanding so little and, being in the hands of the priests of the freedom of speech, we end up accepting as facts, things, happenings and subjects that are the result of poorly developed ideas or, in the misfortunate case, lies with a means.

If you take a journal today and read about any news on the third page, even online, you can go back in time and find it some other day on the second one and sometime back making the headlines. That story eventually will vanish from the tabloid and soon from your memory as well. Which are the important reports? Why some stories go as far as being prize awarded for its true-to-life precision and its impact on the characters, the society or the region involved, as if the others were by that same token worthless or fake? How do we distinguish what to follow and what to let go? In short, what is credible news? Is it that small note on the fifth page that relentlessly stays day after day hibernating before it erupts? Or, is it that other also lost in the middle of the paper that builds momentum by the weeks, gets into people's minds, then into their conversation till it finally breaks through into a decision basis? "My friend told me", "Heard it on the radio", "I read it somewhere", "So many people can't be wrong". We are told to stay informed, to make the best decision. We are not experts on nearly any field, we have to trust. Guess what, the voices and faces on the screen and the loudspeakers are neither experts, their pristine robes and perfect smiles do not make them the 'high priest'.

Once in a while, at strategic social or political times, we have outstanding news: a *leak* by a known person from a concealed source. News to produce an imbalance, to arouse awe. "There is more to come tomorrow," we're told, just as a TV show with seasons and episodes. It is remarkable that we disapprove much more the leak itself than the unveiled truth. We want to know de source, the *squealer*. That informant is regarded as guilty. As to the information itself, well…it is soon forgotten, the *leak* forever engraved in stone.

Then the accuracy, the life span of a story, its truthfulness, its importance for today and the future, pose for us lots of questions. Maybe to every release we should give a full analysis: who is harmed by it? Who benefits from it? Who denies it? Who seems to be sponsoring it? How it will affect us? Please start by treating the news, either official, press or the mass social media, by asking yourself if that will affect you or if it is just gossip as a pastime. Next, size the impact and find what should be done. Next, wait and wait, for nothing extraordinary suddenly happens today. Everything is slowly being cooked. Be a spectator, don´t go with the flow, don't believe all you hear, see or read. Is this a call to anarchy? Is it to reason? Is it an invitation to become the weird suspicious fellow on the team? To become the skeptical one? Be careful, the nest will scent your incredulity, you will place at risk your seat at the common table.

Perhaps life is to continue on its rail, business as usual. News: large, small, astonishing, intriguing, frightening as always. Why bother? "Sip a cup of coffee, relax and in thirty minutes we will inform you to a full detail." You will have the rest of the day to show how much you know about the world, and to discuss with authority every subject of importance today, while the sun keeps circling the earth, mankind warms the planet and our freedom is guaranteed. All sorts of it: freedom of movement, freedom of choice of work, freedom of family size and make, freedom as a consumer, as a hoarder, to vote, to choose sides, to eat, rest, drink, smoke, loiter...and the pinnacle of them all: freedom of thought and speech.

Should we have that freedom? Do we deserve it? Do we honor it? Let me answer that 'I do not know' to the first and 'no' to the latter. As many other things given to us, we embrace and stump on that freedom at the same time, because it is our right, because it is ours and we can do anything to our belongings. Free to be free.

FOUR- Democracy

Democracy:

"From the ancient Greek (demos-people-, kratia-ruling), the ruling by the people. In our time and society, the rule of the majority, either for a government or an organization" (from the 'Facts are Facts' Dictionary)

Also, but archaic,

"Social equality, the nonexistence of classes or distinctions" (from the 'Life's an Utopia' Dictionary)

Democracy the ultimate plateau

We live in a de-moc-ra-cy, the most advanced of all the government systems or so I've read. We hardly know or understand what it is or what it means, but it is certainly something to have, to own. From the moment we are born, we begin to hear about it, democracy. Democracy, we fight for it. We make it our mission to impose this blessing on every land we set eyes upon, in almost the same way that the Franciscans moved in America, northbound of the capital of the New Spain to convert and conquer. At that time, slowly marching in line at the speed of human steps, armed with swords and a few muskets, trailing with mules and recently converted Indians in the role of porters, a couple of priests founded dozens of towns in the name of God. They converted thousands to the new faith and killed two thirds of the population while doing so, although, to be fair, many of the dead died from natural causes, unable to resist the diseases in the tiny form of germs, also brought as an unnoticed weapon to the already unequal fight. The towns, at carefully chosen places, where water flowed and plains allowed for agriculture and grazing, along with some hunting, flourished and became the modern cities we no longer sanctify today. A church became, in all cases, the most important building, they are still standing in our era as a witness of the conversion period. The aborigines are now the strangers to the land, as the new religion and its principles rule the life of the new settlers. In short, the land was taken for the use of the new civilization, crushing in body and mind the other one, despite the little, but forced interbreeding.

Today, as I mentioned, the same thing is happening. We bring armies into different places of the world in the name of God to pursue the conversion to the new religion: democracy, using the same approach: decimate and conquer. We will enslave the living, like those porters, bringing them into our worker's corporate system and we will teach them how to live, how to become productive in freedom, in the arms of the democratic system.

Most of the saved and converted peoples will come from former dictatorships, where the ruler killed as a sport, amassed fortunes that could feed and clothe thousands its entire life, left bare the countryside and created slums where children grew out of the reach of the fundamental needs of life and education. Of course none of that happens in a democracy, for it is the next stage of human evolution.

Oligarchs also fear democracy and are in danger of invasion by our civilization. You could be a Military Junta leader ruling over a land where people are free to live and die as they have always done, with their habits and traditions allowed to be carried on, and poverty as a distinctive feature. No, their lives are not perfect, but perfect is a hard to define position, at the doors of tradition. You are only letting things take the course they are meant to take. You understand modern life and you believe in democracy, but your people would not understand it. They need a guide, the one your fellow soldiers can provide. They know about custom, they rely on their ancient productive ways. You, on the other hand, know about order, economy and progress, and you get along with a few that understand things the same way. Why change? Of course again, none of this happens in a democracy.

Aristocracy is said to be a system where a small group, a privileged one, rules over the rest. Well, as far as I know, just as we moved into the ruling of the people, we ended all aristocracies in the world and now there are no such fortunate groups. Today, democracy has leveled all social classes, we are all rich and fortunate, and no corporations, no millionaires, no aristocratic powers, decide our fate. We, the people of the democracy, rule ourselves.

I am at a loss here. I am confounded with the plutocrats and the aristocrats. Which is which? I don't know the true difference today. Is it just wealth? Is it the remnants of monarchy? Thank God it is a merely historical discussion, since none of those systems or people exist anymore, due to our democracy.

I remember seeing the Queen and the Duchess of somewhere confronted just recently over the WWW –Not world-wide-war, yet to come, just the usual web you know-, but how could that *impossible* happen? They do not occur anymore. I suppose that the actual democracies co-existing with monarchies are just a ruse to lure tourists, since those actors must not really have their castles and huge bank accounts. No, democracy in our civilization, has abolished them all.

The theocrats are also in the retreat. For long the world wanted them out of our lives. The ruling of the living arms of God is diminishing. We have known for centuries –Or is it millennia?- that those that claim to represent the *religare* powers to the highest, are just as human as any, except for the better life they have at our expense. Nonetheless they no longer exist. A few scattered here and there, begging for attention, once more, democracy has taken the strength out of their hands and they no longer control us, thanks be to God.

The examples of the deceased systems can go on and on. The various antidemocratic systems have failed. Only historical ruins remain. The left-standing truth is that finally we have achieved progress, equality, well-being, comfort, freedom and no need for hope, since we have it all, thanks to the establishment of democracy.

Democracy, a word of universal meanings

Once you are in a democracy you don´t need anything, and the word itself stands for everything.

Democracy means free world, the place where you can do almost anything with unlimited chances and opportunities. Democracy means equality, despite how different you may feel from others on your income, education or life style. Democracy is law abiding, because thing are so right that the need to go against your surroundings or neighbors vanishes

Liberté, egalité et fraternité must also be a translation of democracy.

Now, let's go to all the other popular synonyms of democracy: progress, modernity, security, wealth, education, choice, liberty, understanding, brotherhood, ~~establishment & control~~ –I apologize-, community, peace. The whole propaganda package. I probably left out a hundred concepts most people would include. Let's see how democracy works in your mind for everyday language, for everyday life. For instance, let's use the word peace, so important to us in the following sentence:

"We have a troubled country. In yours, do you have **peace**?" "Of course. I live in a democracy."

You can now substitute every word of good available in the dictionary *in lieu* of the word **peace** and you will find the explanation to a universal word: democracy.

Needless to say that we can also use any word arising from an unwanted situation and answer this time with "Of course not. I live in a…" Aren´t we just overdoing the value of it? Democracy is actually a lot less than we claim it to be. It is nothing more than a system to appoint government officials in a *"free"* way, and not so open at that.

Democracy, your right to choose –or so they say-.

This is how your vote works. First of all, the community in power -economic, political or social-, in accordance or in a leverage struggle, chooses who will represent their interests, who will protect their way of life, a handful of people that will uphold their principles. The people they have in mind will differ in personality and image, even on ideas on common subjects, but will always agree on what to shield. These variations in character open the door for the involvement of people, since it is important that the ruler or leader in turn be accepted by the majority, to ease its administration. So, they are presented as candidates for you to vote. Although there may be millions of people, although you may have plenty of options for this or that spot in your local, regional or nation leadership, your opinion is actually not important. You like green? Here is only red and blue. But you get to choose. In the best of cases you may be able to decide over 5 or 6 possible candidates. In the most common scenario only two and, believe it or not, in some instances only one. Your choice is not open. Somebody has narrowed your opinion to a point where you do not even know where that person, you have to vote for, came from. You have no idea who it is, what she or he wants, except to serve you. Ha! I meant to reach the power and serve its masters. What you should be aware of, is that the choices come from the same pool: the system. The people in power appoint for you one of their own, styled for you, appealing, sounding right, as the change you've being waiting for, with the ideas you longed for. You have a candidate.

Things need to be stirred a little bit. Then, a huge and costly apparatus, called the parties –again in some cases two, in others as much as five- are set to oppose each other, to deliver ideas, facts and lies as needed, to reach almost the same goal: your prosperity and well-being. The parties are set nationwide, have distinguishable colors, slogans. Some, claim to be for the people and against the establishment, some for you and in favor of your economy. Very seldom is there someone campaigning for the establishment that, after every period, arrives battered and wishing to leave office.

The parties employ thousands and promote growth for advertising businesses during the campaign. As we know, that is not exactly wealth generation, in the end, is people's expenditure, so that we all get a means to correctly choose. The people within the parties have fierce arguments, they fight first for a place in their own hierarchy, second for a niche in the nation's structure and, as a top goal, for the best spot, namely a candidacy, all for you and your better future. They make a living out of that, but keep in mind that the public wealth and health is never out of their minds, no outside powers or interests move the parties other than us. That's how the birth of options takes place.

One of the big problems of democracy is democracy itself. Face it, it is impossible to let millions of people choose millions of candidates for a position. We have to drop democracy, or shorten it if you like, in order to have a smaller number of choices and, even then, we confront the problem of allowing you to decide. What do you actually know about economy? What about sustainability? What about community needs if you can´t even correctly decide about Home-Ec.? The small but continuous disagreement at home on what to do for the weekend, what repairs the house needs, what schools or courses should your children take and which are the important issues to address over other, because your income, your budget, is limited, are just a fair way to show how ignorant we are on other larger scale problems that a nation faces. No, you cannot choose. It would be crazy to allow you more than to express your opinion. Thus, in the true world, you do not select any one, but you are democratic, because no one is forcing a leader upon you.

In some cases, there is something called a direct vote, where people actually decide on the outcome of the narrowed choice. Millions of votes against millions of votes on a race with the millisecond photo finish. Certainly it gives you the feeling of being in charge. Unfortunately, in some other cases, there is above you a parliament deciding for you or, even worse, a representative whom you did not vote to represent you, and that you do not even know, someone to decide for you, just because the system believes you are not fit to decide. They are not wrong, we are not fit for it. That is why democracy is just propaganda. It also explains why our way of life does not change from one government to the next. It is the same government extended on a renewed face. Same values, same thoughts, same road, same people in power, same poverty, same problems, same life.

Picture for a moment that the power of media, including the new social media, can direct our decision based on truths but also based on lies. Imagine that, by repeating once and again something, we can be convinced about it. Someone with the ability to begin and nurture a lie, a devious thought, could change our world for worse, only because we did not have the judgment to impede ourselves from agreeing on that false and dangerous statement. The same is true for a good idea for social improvement, which could overturn the actual system, to have a government of the people for the people. In any case, to prevent a fallout of our way of life and to preserve the system, we are not supposed to have a true choice. We can be handled against the establishment, the proof of it being that we are handled by and for the establishment. In short, we can be maneuvered, making it a reason to avoid actual democracy and, in turn, set up a fake one.

Let me be *avant-garde* by proposing to grant a daring power to the people that would improve this scarce democracy: the *blanche* vote.

The ballot, in most cases, is set with the prepared options, a person may at will, cross his choice or even write one with the name of an independent runner, because in some countries such is the possibility. One may also decide to annul the vote by crossing more than one option or the whole sheet. Another way to do this is to stay at home and not bother to vote, because neither candidate appeals to you, you don´t believe in independent aspirants or you know that independent stands for "I am wasting my time and yours, playing in a field I am not wanted." Instead of that, think that there is a blank space on the sheet, not to write anybody's name, but simple to cast a vote, a vote of disagreement. Only that this vote implies that if we, the people, vote for it, it will mean. "Hey, we don´t like your options, we don't like your candidates." In that scenario, if the blank votes triumphs, the result would be to disable the candidates for a period as long as the period they expected to be in power and, you guessed it, to have a new election with a new set of candidates. I know, I know, this is costly, but history has shown us that more than once we knew that none of the proposed people was fit for the job. We should at least have the right to say, "Get them all out and bring new ones into the picture," but that is a lot to ask from our meant-to-be-limited democracy, again, it is a dangerous thought. A politician that lost an election will never be regarded as bad as one that was ousted from one. What if we fancy to get rid of them all?

Democracy, the power of the people.

Sometime ago there was a meeting for a series of branches of a company. The reunion was held to decide over the duration of a strike that seemed the only possible way to force the management to discuss certain aspects of the union contract that the lawyers of the corporation had decided to leave out for better times.

The meeting with about 35 representatives from 20 branches, had started with long speeches to convince the assembly of this or that. People were tired after a couple of hours of it, however, every branch had the democratic right to tell and stress to the others their viewpoints and the particular situation that each branch lived. Whether the ideas were fluent or not, whether it corresponded to the issues at stake, each branch could spend as much as 10 minutes to express their anger, grief and a position or solution to the problems. I will not bore you with the details of it. To the fortune of the crowd, some declined their right and only asked for a vote to begin. It eventually came to that.

Before the open vote was done by just naming out-loud the option, these were clearly stated by the representatives that, as we know, were appointed by each and every branch and were taking the position that had been voted before at their factories on a likely meeting. The positions, written on chalk on a blackboard, were simple: a 72 hour strike, an indefinite strike or, strangely, no strike at all. The vote proceeded by asking each branch to vote as their turn came and a mark was added under the choice. When the vote ended, a tie between the 72 hour and the indefinite strike was at 10-10. For a brief moment people spoke at the same time, neighbors would comment on what to do, until someone realized that three postures were on the board, but that only two were voted for.

"Who said no strike?" asked the leader.
"We did," said a man on the middle of the room, standing from his chair and pointing at a coworker of his.
"Well. I must say you have some nerve to vote against your brothers at your factory. You came here with an order. Vote for no strike!" In what seemed a very straightforward thing to do.
"If we do *that*, we will go into indefinite strike, not the 72 hours

we just voted for, and that is worse," the man explained and turned to get some understanding from the rest of the group. "You can't vote different than you were told."

The man explained that the will of each branch could be changed during the meeting and that, precisely, the previous discussion was meant to modify or affirm the idea and proposal they had before coming. Being open minded was not particularly accepted. The decision on what to do came with a vote. Those against the right for them to change their vote raised their hands. The vote shifted to "no strike" and the strike went on for three long months. Nothing to explain, it is the power of the people that puts a dignitary in place and that person should always do what the people want, what the people said or instructed, right?

If we were left out on any decisions in our home town, we would feel powerless and abused. We would find ourselves complaining constantly about the turn of any actions taken by our government. On the contrary, if our vote appointed our governor, then we may sympathize to some extent with the course of events handled by our leader. It is only in our perception. Our vote is merely a match-making exercise.

Democracy, the ignorant majority in power

Why don't we go back to a major problem that comes with our right to decide? We are not irresponsible enough to actually not vote. If you've ever been to a regional meeting held at the town hall or the school cafeteria, in that small head town, you will find that there are at least to opinion trends: the ones from town and the ones from out-of-town. How else could it be? Those living in farms and gravel roads have very different needs from those with the gutter-lined paved streets. A rainy day contrasts umbrellas with sludge, muddy boots with stained stockings. The way ones see life, their goals and expectations, their priorities, is quite different and in some cases opposed to the others. Of course that is what democracy is for, to help us decide what is best, to let the majority impose what is good for everybody. This is true anywhere you go. The majority votes, and it often votes wrongly.

You vote freely but, many times, gregariously. The subject is unimportant to this behavior. You vote on taxes and the use of them, for instance, but you can only see its utility based on what your knowledge allows you to see. You can´t understand the position of your fellow man and, in any case, you will use that majority power to do what is good for you, regardless of what is good for them, because you are ignorant. "No! Didn´t we all agree? Didn't we all think the same?" Yes, Ignorance aligns us all, easily.

We are not experts on every subject that comes across our democratic life. We have our limited education, our limited experience, yet we talk and vote as the appointed appraiser. We do not lean on those who know about the subject at hand. We may listen but, in the end, we will decide what is best for us as individuals, not what is best for the community, simply because we will never resolve against our interests. We will acquire street lamps over repaving country roads because we have our fears and, above all, we are the majority. A windmill that will supply electricity for the town, what harm can it do for the farms? Windmill farms and vineyards can coexist, can´t they? It is for the greater good, the majority needs. Or a highway that will split farmland, how much can it disrupt the operation of a few against the need to commute and speed up of the many? How and where should we dump or treat our residual waters, our solid waste? Where should our clean energy come from? Where should we deplete to ensure our everyday resources? What should we dedicate the outdoors for? Leisure or production? What sort of leisure? Skiing, trek, fishing, hunting, biking? What sort of production? Agroindustry, consumer goods, trash recycling, chemicals?

We are not prepared for most of the decisions we take via a vote, but we feel entitled to. The solution of the system against our ignorance is simple: We are not to be prompted to vote. There is a hierarchy in every household, office, store, warehouse, factory, farm, or church, that holds the power, that possesses the knowledge, needed to guide us, no questions asked, no opinions heard and no votes cast.

Democracy has left me undemocratically speechless, let´s move to something more tangible.

FIVE- Justice

Justice:

"The characteristic of being correct, impartial, fair or reasonable" (from the 'Things Yet to Be' Dictionary)

Justice. Maybe that is what we seek in democracy but, either we are fair and reasonable or, we have the rule of the majority. First discovery: justice and democracy oppose each other, they do not match. I would rather let someone else decide my fate as long as it is fair, wouldn't you?

Justice is a tough one. Maybe if things crumble one day and we bring all of our dogmas –our foundations- before a jury, Justice would probably have in its defense something of this sort:
"There is no prove I was ever there. You cannot charge me with anything related to the end of this civilization. In fact, I have millions of witnesses that will testify on my behalf. People that would fill up this courtroom, even if you held the hearings outdoors! There is not even a hint that I was ever part of that society. I am innocent. I was never there! Truthfully, I am surprised you found me to get me here. I have always been an ideal, nothing solid, never a foundation."

Always an ideal. That is the true nature of justice. For one thing, poverty, for another, discrimination and abuse. In our society there is certainly abuse, it is precisely founded upon it, so that fairness does not exist. If fair is an absent quality so it is justice. Period.
It is nice however, to believe we pursue it and to cherish it as something real, but do not kid ourselves, justice hasn't arrived yet. Stand up, go to the door, open it and see how unfair, how unjust this world is. Turn on your TV or use your phone, tablet or laptop, to approach any and all happenings today, not one where justice is present.

This ideal of justice has made us set up a whole system of codes, regulations and laws. Bills upon bills to tackle the unjust, to have on the bottom line at least the feeling that we got even or, as we say, that justice was served. To do so, we have a conceptual two thirds of our government devoted to law and enforcement, but we fail to foresee every possible abuse and leave, in every rule, enough room, ample voids, to nourish law breakers.

It seems that our nature is not that of the fair. Just for starters, we talk about competition and *that* we do in every aspect of our life, from sports to economy and war. We develop allies. We don't make friends. We suspect our neighbors. We build up leverage. We grow strong to prey on the weak. We prepare ourselves to be the best, to conquer, because there is a jungle out there. We praise the winners. We despise the defeated. We crush those that we do not need, yet we fear everyone. Staying on top is a survival trait. It really is in our nature. Fairness is not.

Who, ever, started this wild and unattainable idea of justice? Why do we long for it? Oh! It just occurred to me that the way we see justice is only in our favor. That must be it! We believe that if things go our way, the world is being fair to us. That if results are soothing to our body and mind then justice is present. We don't care about the fellow next door, about the neighbor beyond our border. We don't mind if justice does not apply for everyone. Often, we will use justice as a reason to intrude in other people's lives, to irrupt in other societies we dislike or we want to loot one way or another. We'll free people from their unfair rulers, with an angle: the one to sack.

In a very romantic way we recall the 17th and 18th century pirates and their ships. We almost iconize them, despite the point, that at the time they openly displayed their unjust nature. Today, as our civilization boards other, it is carefully disguising our piracy. We are there to help, to bring justice. Ha! How can we deliver something we don't even have?

Justice comes along the lines of community, of brotherhood, but we have a long way to travel before we ever get it. We are selfish, we are abusive. Our religions try to impose, or just plainly convince us, that we are a family with an almighty father, a dedicated and flawless mother, and sisters and brothers that live in peace caring for each other. Once a week we reinforce this thought, but being competitive is pumped in our veins the rest of the time. We then cheat and deceive, but we win. We win in love and war and in everything in between. Brotherhood is set aside, since competition is the true value of our times. Peace is also on hold.

Will we ever live in justice? Maybe not. So far we have accomplished a system strong enough to support a certain degree of fairness to a certain amount of people, the problem being that it comes at a high cost in our society. We impose on ourselves a series of individuals to act as referees on our doings. We rely on them to keep our society in one piece. Many times we disagree on their ruling but in the end we accept their line of behavior, after all we also need to be protected from others. It is this duality, enforcement and protection, the way we have designed our road to justice. Not bad for a start, someone would say, but too far to make us a justice-proud society. Maybe there are examples out there of communities that prove me wrong. Maybe you are part of a movement that peacefully and smoothly lives in justice, good for you. As for the millions at the waiting room, the struggle will go on, because faith, hope and patience will not do.

"Hey watch it!" An old man complaining about a teen that had just banged against his chair, next to the pool at breakfast, on a tropical resort. The boy didn't even bother to turn.
The young fellow was with a couple of friends staying at the same hotel, I believe on a vacation/tuition combination, with their Spanish teacher.
The guys kept pushing and playing during the buffet and their tutor seemed upset, willing to do something and not quite

getting there. Almost at the end of my meal, a kid brushed by me and my glass fell to the floor. He stopped.

"Hey!" I called, "Please, be nice." He looked at me as if waiting for more to come, then I added, "You know? Nothing wrong happens when you're nice." He then approached me and started to pick up the pieces, but a waiter came to finish the job. He slowly left, head down.

In the afternoon, his teacher came to me, introduced himself and said, "Thank you. How simple really, 'be nice' I'm going to use that from now on. We always try 'behave', 'behave', 'do this, do that', but this is it 'be nice.'"

Maybe it is the behavior, the value, we should ask for.

Lately, organizations, corporations and even governments have embraced a system of core values and statements of vision and mission, I believe in order to develop a pleasing image to improve *sales and market share*. The most common values are integrity, innovation, teamwork, excellence, leadership, quality, performance, trust and respect, all of them aiming at being a strong competitor. Fairness or justice are not among the values. Who would want to be fair? It's insane!

I regret to have brought a concept that does not define our West-Civ.

Being fair goes far below from being nice. Being nice implies doing something for others as simple as not shouting at a dinner, respecting a line at a ticket booth, keeping your numbered seat at a game instead of seeking to 'improve' your view, lifting your pets feces, mowing your lawn, getting a shower before a long bus ride to your hometown or all of those things that I can't think of, but that you already thought, things that bother you on the street, the supermarket, the road, your office, your shop or the outdoors, that you don't do, but others do.

On the other hand being fair can make you a motionless bystander when something happens to others. If you do not intervene, fair enough.

You don't have to help to be fair. Being fair is respecting the other and must certainly not abusing the other.

Nice is too much, but why isn't fair in our core values?

SIX- *Égalité*

Égalité, egalitarian

"Qualité d'etre égal". "A core value in our society, about people being all equal and having the same rights" (from the '...seriously?' Dictionary)

The equality of classes

Stated as a slogan for two countries at the end of the 18th century, this concept of equality strikes us as one of those sales we will not buy, as one of those offers we would like to take, and even embrace, but that we know it to be unreal. At least so would the idealistic romantics of humanity would say. In fact, I know many people who believe that humans are not equal at all, that we should deserve nothing else but the treatment that arises from difference. So then, just to humor the proposal from the basis of our civilization, we can go into it, taking a look at the real world before we go back into the cozy dream: *l'égalité*

People are not born equal in any way, do not live equal in any way and not even when dead are we equal. Starting at the price a funeral home charges you to be removed from circulation with dignity, respect and thoughtful memories ...well, there are qualities and qualities: raw wood and brass, carpets and dirt floors, bright and somber wakes, a mourners list, limousines, speeches, just before the remains are placed into a mausoleum or...you get the picture.

There is something called the upper class, far away from everybody, that looks down into the world as something detested, though needed at the same time. The future looks promising, since the intelligent machines are about to take over on all those needs. It is just a matter of time, suddenly that class will no longer need anyone. They will be amongst themselves equal or sort of equal. Not an anticipated happy ending. No, happiness will not reign even there, for ambition for power and wealth never ceases. They wonder why on earth there had to be that mass of uneducated, unrefined people, just outside their walls and crowding the streets, leaving a foul smell floating. They wonder why they have to drive with their windows rolled up and the air conditioning running, instead of breathing the scent of an autumn morning or that of a spring afternoon. Some long for a moment of true peace and calm with the privacy of just being alone, no guards no security.

A friend of mine –it is always someone else's story, not ours, so not mine-, a friend of mine comes from those families that today are not as powerful or wealthy as they used to be three or four generations ago. His family owned more that one of those properties where the very rich were surrounded by the very poor, where the very poor lived in barracks or huts, had no last names and their given names were precisely, given...by their masters. His great grandfather used to be forced by the family to run a farm, practically set on a marsh, where mosquitos would cloud the air during the summer time and the never ending buzzing would drive a man crazy. That place had no slaves to do the work, instead it had prisoners kindly lent from the nearby penitentiary. This 'poor' man was almost sent in punishment to deal with the people and nature at the same time, just to keep the business going. He would always return withered and ill, it would take him a good deal of the winter at his parental state to recover, before having to go back in the spring, to stay the rest of the year making that mill work, amongst "those people".

There are, I am sure, examples like this dating back to that time for all sorts of businesses: oil, mines, agricultural fields, factories and the construction of the early infrastructure, including railroads, marine ports and dams. Today the heirs of that legacy do not have to suffer the close encounters, from the distance they can handle their investments, provided a good old fashioned foreman is in place.

Not everything goes right appertaining to this class, there are worries too. Although it seems that all the needs are covered, it turns out that new needs arise including the competition among the equals, who want to be different, be more, to be not so equal. Wine is wine except to the sommelier and to the snobs that pretend to know about the subtle distance in taste from one red to another red.

The struggle to be different, more sophisticated, excentric, more refined, guides this class, like any other, into deceit, friendship, alliances, envy, selfishness and egotism, just to mention a few of our most distinguishable traits as humans. Our economic or social condition does not change our nature. There are and arise unattained goals, unsolved fears, permanent phobia, but of course also the good things as love or solidarity. There in our nature we are truly equal.

It is not hard to see that the common guy has today at his reach what the upper class of a century ago could not even imagine to have. The comfort of life today would prove a luxury to that time. Then, progress will bring to everybody the advantages that wealth gives to some today. But of course you want it now.

Maybe you would want to be like those people. In that case it proves that there is no equality between you and them. Maybe you do not want at all to be like them. It still proves a difference. Finally, you could be them and certainly understand that there is a difference.

How does this fit into the so called equality in terms of rights and opportunities, in terms of social and political conditions? Well, it doesn't fit.

There is something called the middle class, which amounts, depending on the western country under study, from 20 to 80% of the population, just a narrow range. This class is the buyer and consumer of everything from goods to concepts. This class is the proper field to sell democracy, freedom and justice, but also equality. They can open the door from their house and see the world just as it should be: equal and fine. They all have jobs. They all have dreams –limited but dreams-. They all have weekends to relax. At work, during the daily breaks, they can discuss about the new electronic devices available on the market or they can debate about the Sunday's game or games and certainly discuss the political outcome of the forthcoming election. They can argue about telephone or internet rates, the gym and Pilates best hours, the best coffee shop, deli or SPA, mortgage periods, insurance coverage, motor-vehicles down payments, the summer vacations –and the winter holidays as well-, college options for their kids and savings accounts. You have the right to plan.

The dreams of this middle class, for the most, are engulfed in one word: climb. People want to be more, want above all to have more. They want to, for starters, to beat their parent's finish line, to have accomplished better. Marketing tells them what to want and what to reach for, along with their everyday comparison at work and in their neighborhood, the benchmarking of life. Status is important and it is measured -or so it looks like-, with the amount of useless things we collect, from credit cards to tools or personal gadgets, of course our assets in the bank, the making of our cars and the size and location of our home. Being busy is also part of the scene.

In this world segment, there is certain ease that allows you to forget the ones at the top and the other ones at the bottom. You have the chance to think, to be a critic, to speak out. Well, no wonder you can buy any concept, any social trend. Hello! You are manageable. Your thoughts can be controlled, your ideas planted, your goals set, but maybe it is what you actually want. The larger the middle class is, the easier it feels to be equals, to feel that opportunities are there for all, but there aren't.

There is the lower class, where gardening during the weekend or fixing the garage door is not an option, where the comfort zone does not exist. This lower class is despised by the other two and often by themselves. It is the most inconvenient life a person could have, certainly a truly unwanted circumstance. There is no need to deny its existence. There is no need to deny that our perfect society produces individuals scrounging for food, clothing and shelter, hoping to at least get the first and the latter on a not so irregular basis. They represent the truth of our civilization, the failure of it. Our failure.

Since we cannot deny it and since the portrayed idea is not unknown to any of you, this class is the living proof of inequality. About the causes, we may discuss a lot depending on our political *clichés*, our religious dogmas or simply our oversized smug viewpoints. We will never accept it as a failure of our system. We may attempt to cover it under the laws of nature and its never inaccurate statistic comportment. If there is up, there must be down, right? The so famous 80/20 Pareto´s law was precisely born upon the observation of nature – plantation productions by the way- but also on the observation of property –here I am not so sure it is natural-. Then, why should it be strange that 20% of the people on earth and in our civilization possess 80% of the wealth whereas 80%...you do the math. But when we step at the bottom of the ladder we can affirm there is something else going on. Something unacceptable.

What is to be expected from these margined groups? What solutions come to mind? Their life begins in a hole excavated by their ancestors while trying to ascend. It continues in distress, discomfort, illness, ineducation, along the side of petty crime that soon escalates within *normality* into higher deeds, mostly coming from need, from survival.

One day, on those coffee breaks where we discuss the world and the "I would do this" and "I would do that," the "It's so easy. Why can't they do it? Schmucks!"… On one of those days, the subject was precisely poverty and crime. At one point, one stated that we didn't understand any of that because we were all "well off", but if the moment came, where our family would not have food on the table, we would steal either the food or something to get it. Our values and our integrity would all fall and we would adapt to the new reality, starting by blaming others of our situation and explaining that we had no choice, that the unusual circumstances had forced us to act as we wouldn´t otherwise, but that we remained the same.

I can add a lot more, merely to end up saying that poverty and crime have the same birthdate as opulence and human abuse from one citizen to another, the line when one deprives the other from his rights, and through machination, of its scarce assets.

Did I mention we fear them, the poor? What remains to be answered is if that fear just comes from the threat they represent to us, because they want something we have – remember they have nothing to lose- or because we know that we, the rest of society, are the cause of that unfortunate circumstance they live on. Regardless of all thoughts, the system is not providing a level ground of opportunities. It is again propaganda in favor of those who have the power and means to disseminate it –money and mass media, certainly-.

It's the poor's fault

Besides carrying the load of lacking most of what a dignified living stands for, the poor also have to bear the guilt of their condition. It's their fault to be poor. The opportunities are there for everyone, right? Haven't you heard or read about incredible CEO's of successful companies that started their venture on the garage of their parental house, did not finish a college education and created this or that paramount invention? All right, if I am correct, they had a house with a garage. They had one way or another, parental support. They decided to give up their college studies because they could choose. They had the opportunity.

Once in a while, extraordinary things are done by certain individuals, but when we consider a statistical trend there is nothing scaled by the hundreds, thousands and, obviously, not by the millions, which is the real goal of opportunity. Only a few succeed, the mass remains hoping but failing or not attempting at all, because food and shelter are not there.

Our society makes the victim feel guilty, makes the poor look responsible for their fate, although their upbringing was more accidental than planned or proposed, dried fallen leaves at the mercy of strong winds. It is nevertheless the easy way out for the rest of society, because it is not our fault, not our doing. We can turn the eyes elsewhere and pretend they do not exist or just regard them as the burden of our community. They did not strive enough, I don't know, it's the poor's fault.

The fading of classes

Following the world known tactic to divide and conquer, classes are being washed away from our mind by all the arising, though forever existing, needs and hurdles of the minorities, side by side to our natural differences.

First about the natural variations. We are not suit for every job or occupation, because we have a wide range of motivations, gifts and physical qualities and disabilities as well. Opportunities cannot be the same, neither can outcomes, but a certain solid base is needed for us all: the true chance to match our person to our attainable goal. That is the only thing we can ask for.

About the minorities, keep in mind that a small group here, may be large group elsewhere, it is circumstantial. More than often, these groups are present in all of the above three classes and suffer different ways of discrimination that tend to make us forget about the classes. You can either be set apart by ethnicity –recall the last racist remark you heard, just yesterday-, age, gender, sexual preference and behavior – again, think about the crude but easy comment you heard at the grocery store last Saturday-, nationality or origin –maybe you are the targeted minority-, occupation –some professions should actually be banned-, weight –a classic one-, height, dexterity or dullness, being impaired, suffering from an illness, exercising a diet, having a rare hobby, even how you speak, - your language type, use and pronunciation-, dressing taste, political inclination –any particular party you hate?-, religion, the association you belong to, the club you attend, your chosen sport or any other differences you may want to add about your common life, not excluding the use of your right hand over your left, really? You are struck from all directions: from the perimeter, above and below. You are distracted, even at your will, from wider, more fundamental matters. You struggle in your particular world of problems, prompted and carefully followed by the professional and amateur media, while the original obstacle that is truly bothering you, the inequality of the classes, the fact that they exist, fades away. We are easy marks to be set apart by our endless, multiple, unimportant, differences.

It is not that I want to clash classes. No, I just want them to vanish, to become one. There are others that, at their own discomfort and risk of security, want the classes to exist. Obviously, despite the inconveniences, there is a gain in maintaining things as they are, as if saying "let them fight, make them work but don´t let them die…only some, if needed," "make them compete, make them wound each other and make them strong enough for their appointed purpose: our earnings."

Every time then, that your attention is set on the small fires here and there, the true red hot charcoal keeps smoothly burning, with a glow that delights a few, a very few. Your voice is apparently heard to solve those little things brought upon you as both a nuisance and a mind filling task that, if ever solved, would leave you with the primal problem still present.

The second law of thermodynamics

The what?

To put it plainly, this true law –not the so called laws of economics that never cease to surprise us with its inconsistencies and unrelated cause-effect -, this law states that every process in the universe –of which we are part and not the center, in case you wondered-, every happening in life, tends to spend energy and come to an equalization with the surrounding, always at a lower energy state called equilibrium. This is a natural law.

Another way to explain it is that every action has a driving force that is depleted during the process. Such as a river flowing down hill, where the driving force is the potential energy due to the pull of gravity. The river goes as far as the sea. There, having no other way to go further down, its water reaches equilibrium, showing as a flat surface. Height determines the potential. Once at sea level there is no more potential and –here is the most important part of the law- the process is not reversed as a natural act, the river will not flow upwards –you don´t say!-.

By that token, assets in our world should point to an equilibrium, to the point where there is no potential. The use of force to take money from the rich –called robbery- couldn´t be more natural. It is just the power of nature adjusting the system, equalizing it, setting equilibrium. What causes migration? Well the balancing of that system. Do people migrate from the first world to the first world? Not really. Do they migrate from the first to the lesser ones? Not really, unless it is for as long as it is needed to plunder to emptiness those other worlds. The natural migration is the opposite, where over-the-time accumulated momentum is driving it to balance. According to another law of thermodynamics –zero at that- , the individuals of the first world are already at equilibrium amongst themselves, nothing to steal form one another, no gifts to expect. There, we are equals.

In the beginning there was some sort of equilibrium, just as the one the aborigines of North America stated they had with their surroundings before modernity literally railroaded them. That equilibrium was offset by our system creating a high temperature zone and a low temperature zone or, if you may prefer, a wealthy side and a poor side, creating an unbalanced situation that holds even today, placing in danger of cooling the hotter zone and warming the colder one. You understand what I am getting at, some will believe in it some will not. Never mind, the time will come when that heat wave will strike cold and end the motion of the system at its departure point when everything was just warm.

Let's leave this behind and move unto laws and forces we all grasp.

Get your tag ready

Mr. Simmons a veteran manager at a factory arrived one day early morning and received an unwelcome surprise.

"Good morning Mr. Simmons," greeted the guard at the door, "please, show me your ID and swipe it through the reader."
"My ID?"
"Yes as of 12 o'clock last night, everyone has to show an ID before coming in," said the smiling man.
"What? What for?"
"Just the instruction. Your ID please, Sir."
"Seriously? An ID? But you know who I am!" patience fading, "I am your boss. *I am* the boss."
"No exceptions Mr. Simmons, your ID please."
"Do you realize how ridiculous you sound...Ben?" After a quick look at the body tag on his chest. "Mr. Simmons your ID?" But he reached for his wallet and said, "Here," while handing him his driver's license.
"Not this one, Sir. Your corporate ID," said the calm man in uniform.
"Well...I don´t have it with me. Just open the door."

"Can't."

"Call your superior please," and making an effort to recall the name, "Mr. Robins. Call Mr. Robins."

"He will tell you the same. You have to show your corporate ID Mr. Simmons."

About to snap at him or himself, the manager started to digit his cellphone, to reach someone to clear the situation, when a knock on the just rolled-up window drew his attention again, "You have to move your car. You cannot stay here at the entrance," said smiling Ben.

He parked away from the door and dialed a number. A machine answered and proposed a dialing menu. No! He needed to speak to someone, not leave a message.

Welcome Mr. Simmons to system land, a place where speedy servers decide your fate. Before the machines we have become equals. No urge can be conveyed, no feelings apply. There is no way to lure the electronic brain and have it working for you. Now you are a pulse, another number in the line. The just-answered phone call will be placed on hold, just as anybody else's, in case the auto menu is not to your liking or needs, or you –as you actually- need to speak to a human. In addition, the human will answer you as an extension of the machine, a talkative system interphase. You are lost, because there we are equals. Next time, get your tag ready.

Alliances and guilds

There is nothing so common as alliances and guilds. You may call them associations, partnerships, chambers, unions, groups, clubs or related names, pursuing always the benefit for those summoned, for those called to the brotherhood. What we do not fail to see is that we are surrounded by the others, the ones that do not belong to our alliance, as if our group was meant to profit over them. We are not wrong. By grouping, we defend ourselves from the rest of the society because we need to, and once in a while we attack that

society. We actually try to profit from it, to gather from it
something just in our favor. Every human group does it. Our
civilization too.

The creation of allies divides humanity and society, favoring
inequality within our known-to-be-equalitarian civilization.
Moreover, it differs widely from friendship, because friendship
involves affection, not interest. Thus, it is with a sad mood that I
find that our civilization does not make friends, it has allies with
rules and written commitments of loyalty, exchange and
support. We help each other by the book. We have each
other's back. We show muscle together when needed. We
fake smiles when we meet and carefully spy on each other
because we have no trust. Our pursuit is not always the same
and is not always clear, because deep inside we are not
equals.

There is so much to protect because there is so much abuse.
The abuse of our unequal system. Fishermen protect their
ranges, their quotas, their open seasons rights. Factory unions
fight for wages, lunch time, leisure time, safety and health
care. Farmers associations strive to market their product for
their yearly marginal gains. Automobile makers associations
lobby for better tax exemptions. Consumer products
companies and commodities manufacturers chambers
maneuver for another type of exemptions, the health and
environmental respective regulations, the free market act.
Professional's associations struggle for a dignified and better
remunerated acceptance in society. Construction companies
groups discuss better opportunities, larger projects, ampler
time-tables and higher profits. The common ground to all of
this is abuse, either that someone is protecting himself from it
or that someone is imposing it. Our equal society at work.

Ethnic groups

An update on race, you don't have to be a minority for it to
be a problem. Does our civilization present the same face to

every ethnic group? Same treatment? If you belong to a minority your answer is an immediate, no. If you have the skin color that the system has accepted for centuries –decades if not to argue-, then you are on the fast lane, otherwise you are in trouble and are bound to be set apart, that is if you are not already segregated and confined.

In some of our countries the surviving aborigines have special rights, some above the rest of the population, but it is more an act of marketing image than true consideration or favor. Their looted land will never return to them. They curse those days when the wooden ships, loaded with steel cannons, appeared in the horizon.

Again, there are some cases worth mentioning of individuals that fulfilled the unreachable dream. Again a tree does not make a forest, just remember it is the forest we are talking about, when considering equality. Don't fool yourself, from the bus station, the bank, the coffee shop, the grocery store and your job itself, nobody treats everybody in the same way, color matters.

Women's rights

What in the world am I thinking? I so much discriminate women as to leave them outside or in the last of my thoughts? Perhaps. Perhaps absent minded, maybe just on purpose. Maybe the last line of inequality that our civilization tends to forget, but that you will remember as a material proof of nonexistent *egalité*.

SEVEN- Productivity

Productivity:

"In industry, the measured output per time unit. Also, the total output. Often confused with yield or efficiency, where the output is compared to input or the resources needed. In social life, the achievements of an individual" (from the 'Such is Life' Dictionary)

The core value, your performance

There are core values missing in corporate statements, productivity is one of them, although it is the essential principle. We want you all to be a team, to innovate and to observe, at all times, all of the other values, just to be productive, because the corporate's output is the true goal. If the output grows so do the profits, assuming the contribution and the rest of the economic considerations are in place.

Corporations consider at least four assets: money, machinery, knowledge and humans. Of these, the hardest to control is that of humans, but fortunately we turn out to be of a predictable nature. A team of psychologists, ergonomic and industrial engineers, doctors, architects, lawyers and social workers, put their knowledge to work, to deliver a product called the working environment, perfectly mated to the chosen human profile. We are carefully picked, analyzed, put through a test before being submerged in our working place. We, the ones that used to be called the human machinery are now regarded as a corporate's resource or even a capital. We are an asset to the industry, we are an asset even as bureaucrats. This resource is then accommodated in the working place for only one reason: productivity.

You like your job? Good if you do. It means you were correctly chosen and trained. Is not your safety or comfort that matters, it is the output you generate. If you are happy, your output is of better quality and greater quantity. It's a win-win situation, they will tell you and you will believe it and embrace it, because you have also been conditioned for it. It is because of this conditioning that you will not be bombarded with the word productivity. Instead, you will have values that resemble your human values, it will remind your companionable instinct as being part of something, of a group that will protect you and make you proud as well of your common achievements.

A safety concerned corporation measures its accident prevention efficiency in a quotient of lost days vs. working days, not if Mr. Perlx or John had an injury or a lost finger. At the end of the fiscal year, if the said ratio is not that good, but the revenue improved 7%, you will hear the CEO stating that the company had an outstanding year, despite the eye lost by Mr. Sanchez in the third quarter. If however, you have a cero accident record, but a 1% decrease in revenue, then the CEO could probably start looking for a job due to a disastrous year. You see, the human machines are as replaceable as any other. We are as any component: specified, chosen, acquired or leased for the job and eventually replaced. We have to be oiled, cleaned and repaired, maintained in a word. We are an asset meant to be productive.

Performance is a team work done by you, the machines you control, the resources you manage or simply use and the coordinated labor you have with your colleagues or fellow workers. Our performance is measured in product output per time unit, but also in resources employed or consumed. If by chance you are working shifts, then either openly or closed, your team is compared and continuously competing against the other shifts. Performance is carefully followed. Your team is hustled to outrun the other. Your *carrot* –unbelievably the term is used today in the corporations of our modern civilization- is to be recognized as the best achievers in the news board, a picture featured on the third page of the company's newsletter or, in some cases, to be posted as the worker of the month.

Perhaps you have been summoned, along with your wife, at the CEO's annual brunch at his house, but on the lawn – portable toilets at your disposal, you will only see the house from the outside and long for such a status-, where only the best employees are invited once in a lifetime. A glass of champagne -which you don't really like because you are more into beer-, a roll of some salmon sushi type appetizers, followed by a big meal, including things you have never eaten before, will be the frame for your leader's voice, congratulating you for a job well done and launching you into a better next year, full of new tasks, new challenges and greater achievements. You are set to go.

Once a year, that same CEO is summoned to face the real managers: the board. There, the share-holders, in person or represented, will ask dozens of questions and will discuss several issues that will meet or not an agreement. Of course every subject agreed will be conveyed as an order to the employee called the CEO. There is one goal that will have a consensus: a 5% annual increase in revenue, at least. In those meetings the core values will not be addressed because they are not important. Again my mistake, productivity hidden in the revenue increase is the only value to consider.

There are then two battle fields for the company; the open market with its competitors, where Integrity as a whole and in every employee is of the highest importance, then the inner field, within the walls of the business, where high performance, strong productivity and big yields are the desired language.

Interestingly, loyalty seems to be absent, but the very common team-player is fundamental to the operation. Personnel dissolve in the team effort, become one, with a coordinated impulse to be productive.

At the same time that core values shape the policies within and the image to the outside, mission statements try to make the enterprise acceptable to society by including some sort of usefulness, but always pointing out the benefit of its stake holders. Never will you find a mission drafted just for the community, although both, owners and society, will always show in the wording. Not to be surprised, since the needs of the people are the engine for sales and growth. Products must be needed in order to sell. Sometime a void is filled, some other a competition is started. If by any chance the fulfillment of a need is not profitable, then it will not be covered, the company will not be born or the product will not reach that remote place.

In the vision creed, leadership and greatness will be present in the majority. This should make the team players a part of something important, something to stand proud. It boosts the need for achievement. It gives an individual the opportunity to do as a group what could never be done alone, to belong to a gold medal relay by performing any actions –simple or complex- under those colors. It is being part of a bigger creation and feeling vital.

What can I say? Be somebody, be productive.

Productivity bonus

Nothing fits better than being rewarded, constantly compensated for your efforts and achievements. One way is to get a bonus. If you are on the top places at the management, but for some DNA reason you are not part of the founding family, you may get a retribution through the gift or low cost purchase of some tiny shares of the company you will devote your life to. This increases your earnings, but above all, the feeling of belonging, your skin is forever dyed with the company colors.

It may happen that you are not meant to be a part of the top crew. You can still have a bonus. Do not expect a quality or a safety bonus, because those are your responsibility. Instead, expect a productivity one.

"What do you want to get for a 5% increase in productivity?" you may be asked, but don't dare answer, it is only a rhetorical question.
"No answers? You don't know what you want? Tell me. Let's make a deal. It's a win-win situation. You give me more I give you more."

To be thoroughly correct in your answer and your targets, you would need to have access to the financials of the company or, at least, to the break-even point of the product or production line being discussed, otherwise, you cannot answer. Assuming you do have a carefully thought answer, you would have to decide on a percentage, that magic number between zero and a hundred percent of the extra profit your 5% productivity will produce. Now, don't get too excited, your number should never be above 2 or 3%, unless you want to be considered greedy. That percentile is, of course, to be divided among your team, either in a fair distribution or in a prorated one. Again don't jump into sweet conclusions, since you will, sooner than later, find out that an increase in productivity not necessarily means a higher profit, it depends on how you manage to increase production. Did all your variable costs remain the same? Did your fixed ones? OK, you went through all that and there is no doubt, your production increase means more money for the company. Still don't count on it, it could probably turn out that your idea meant a change in the machinery that someone up there will interpret as a productivity gain due to the machinery not you. Maybe it was that chemical added to the process. Maybe that lube oil. Maybe the layout change. Maybe whatever. No matter if you signed the deal, there will always be a way to avoid paying you in the court of law. Moreover, one big question will arise if all said it's done: for how long?

What did you expect? That you or your mates would become shareholders by getting a bite at the profits forever? No. Your bonus will be like for this month or the quarter and once it's over, it will get back to the same question or the one that follows.

"What do you want to get for a 5% increase in productivity?" Don´t answer right away, look like disoriented, and finally say, "We will do our best," then perhaps you will receive a bonus, an unexpected bonus to fuel your loyalty and feel that Christmas came early –no harm intended on the Christian analogy-. You will get a tiny reward, disproportional to the gain achieved.

Comfort zone

Among our first world countries, where democracy has settled and the good life is in progress, that middle class I mentioned earlier, will accomplish the dream: they will have the life of comfort, no stress, no anxiety, no further needs, your balanced performance, but oh no, no! That is a sin against productivity. If you feel fine and your goal has been reached -even as a society- then how can I make you more productive? The answer is that I must not allow you to feel well, must not let you fulfill your dream.

At work I will check if everything is alright with you and your colleagues, if so, I will implement a plan to disrupt your happiness, feeling at ease and comfort. I will bully you with the new idea about "the comfort zone".

"You´re fine? Well, you shouldn't be! You don't want to be more?" Of course you probably would like to appertain to the leading group, but you know is a long shot –sorry for the hunting or war analogy-. It is almost impossible, besides you are doing fine so, why bother? Someone wants you to bother. You got your objective? Well, go for more, because I need it, because the corporation wants it. You are a disgrace if you remain in your comfort zone. I want more. I mean *you* want more. Your target –again a hunting or war analogy- must be higher.

Once we have tackled the middle class, now that people talk comfortably about the negative aspects of being comfortable, then we move along the economic pyramid and, every time we see someone enjoying life, we throw the epithet "comfort zone" and demand people to get away from it "Do something! Of course you don't improve. You are in your comfort zone!"

What's wrong with wanting a simple B or C performance-life full of comfort?

Productivity contest

There are several industrial products such as boilers, cooling towers, compressors, process instruments that, to be manufactured, still need true manpower –I got it wrong? Humor me anyways-.

One day, at the yard of one of this companies, a group of people were assembling, making, pallets. Before noon break, the new employee had managed to produce 20% more than its pals.
"You're doing fine. First day uh?" a not so friendly looking guy said.
"Yeah. I could do more," he answered while eating a sandwich -roast beef at that-.
"You *could* do less," the other man said and squared him in the eye. And before the reply, added "We can *do* more, but there is no use. You want to impress our Sup? Make us look bad? Leave it, son."

Manpower will determine pallets, dresses sawn and, yes, compressors or high quality cars. Are we getting the best performance from that labor? Wake up! Who´s in charge here?

Productivity will always be at stake if people cease to compete. Is your shift more productive that the other two or three? What does the weekly and monthly chart show? Was yesterday's output better than today's?
I have seen shift crews collude to maintain productivity at a

certain level. I have seen some other cases where, at the end of the shift, the process parameters are upset to unable the next workers to compete. In the end, they all agree not to stress themselves, to cooperate, for a reasonable output. A sin? Only a few will accept that. Only a few. Oh! You included, my apologies. I am with the sinners.

The obsolete

Productivity faces a major problem, namely, quality along with durability. If things last long enough to become somehow permanent in our lives, then we have no need to replace them, to renew them. Back in the old days a fridge would last longer than its owners. Cars would be built so tough that, in some places, shows called demolition derbies were possible. How about a solid wood desk as compared to MDF or LDF board one? Maybe I am having delusional ideas of long lasting objects, but there is a fact that today's productivity, which is the main engine of profit, needs things to be replaced.

Your computer platform works fine? Well, here is a new one to replace it along with new gadgets that only work on the new platform. You have to replace it, erase it or upgraded at a new cost. Got a phone? Here is the new 7.8.XZ.4567 version. It's a smash! Yes, all society can be fooled by that. A power drill that lasts under a year. A weed eater that gets you through one summer-fall period. A light bulb that lasts unless it gets a tiny strike while lit, maybe not covered in the guarantee. Things are out of our lives a little sooner than we would like.

On the other hand, there are objects that we discard while still useful –cars included by the way-, why? Because we are told to. How? They are obsolete!

It has been pounded, nailed in our brains, to be as modern as possible, to be innovative. We don't look well of others that drive an old vehicle –three or four year old are accepted-, that wear shoes to the end, that sew torn mittens for next winter, that show the same overcoat over and over again – just like that red one with the big buttons, that your aunty wore to every family reunion, yes, that one, the felt-like, that smelled rotten under the rain-. We have been convinced to see all of that as obsolete, so industry can provide us with the new.

The vogue in electronics is quite peculiar. After a trend of miniaturization we are growing back up: headphones, cell phones, computers, are an example. We downsized, now we reverse. We bought then, we buy now.

The new improved, better than before whatsoever –please feel free to replace the last word for your product- Let's try again. The new improved, better than before, our best ever…powered by the obsolete! Get yours *today* at your local…

Let's make a deal

Not exactly lately but, in humanity's long run it can be said, recently. Yes recently some sort of moral took over business, from the ether came a new way of doing things, where both parties implied were to win, to make a profit either in solid coins, well-being, comfort, or some other type of a practical, seizable, retribution. Everyone would be happy under the new way of conducting business and worker-employer relations. Shouldn't always be as that? Shouldn't we at all times get something as worthy in return? I guess not, but for the first time it is proposed to us. Let's make a deal.

EIGHT- Competitiveness and the free market

Competitiveness:

"The quality of being able to compete; the willingness or enthusiasm to do it and succeed, either for individuals, organizations or countries" (from the 'Seventeen and a Half Ways to Improve Your Life' Dictionary)

The competitive corporation / the competitive nation

It is not enough to be productive or even highly productive, you must also be competitive. In the open market of the free world…Wait! What am I talking about? There is no open market and there is no free world, however, there is a market and a world, although some would argue about the world.

I was saying that, in the open market of the free world, sales are a fierce competition. One of quality, low cost, of geographical reach capability, logistics and marketing. If you are good at all of these…congratulations! You are competitive. If competitiveness has to do with an attitude - or we think-, in the world of business has to do with the fact of being successful, disregarding your attitude. You could be competitive by chance because in your country salaries are low, because you are located wall to wall with your buyers, because you share a sea or a bay, because your country sits on oil fields or has other means of cheap energy supply, maybe also because your raw materials are open mined –just scraped at the surface, in case you were wondering- or a river crosses your land. Yes, you are right, every company and country, even every individual at some point, has some type of advantage over its competition. That is a fair conclusion to something that the free market of the free world regards as unfair. Instead, we must level the ground. We must have the same opportunities for every contestant. Well not exactly, in fact we must foresee the advantages of others in our competition field and assure to erase them. If we are powerful enough we will apply market rules to be more competitive. You are right, our civilization sets the rules to unbalance trade in our favor. So what? The benefits of being us.

Rules can come with many faces: an import tax, a trade tariff, a health concerned embargo, a human rights prohibition, a wilderness or environmental protection bill, a global warming issue, an exclusion from a free trade agreement, the trade agreements as such or the safety cargo regulations of roads, railroads, planes and ships, are among the most common.

To every measure, there is a countermeasure: a subsidy or tax exemption, an unclear merchandise code, a UNC or NGO certification of health, a socially responsible award, a Green donation, carbon credits, bilateral agreements or joint ventures, being the usual.

It's a world of lawyers, the world of make believe, where our image is only what we can prove it to be, legally, unequivocally prove it. You thought you had the best technology, the best manpower, the finest raw materials, the lowest energy cost, the swiftest logistics and now, now you need the best lawyers and marketers to dodge or pass successfully through every hurdle placed by your competition in the free market. How is that for free?

Sometimes the governments, in order to boost their economy, will take actions to promote growth of their companies and production activities, detrimental to foreign opposition. In other circumstances, companies will lobby strong enough through Chambers or Associations to arrive at the same goal. Of high concern it comes that some corporations will fold their flags and even change their names to go global and use every set of rules in every country or trade to profit above the other, money talks, Return-On-Investment rules.

As for the countries, propelled by their own thoughts or those of their corporations, trade zones have been seeded all over the world. In every case, the strongest nation establishes the rules of engagement to profit more than the others on the so called mutually fruitful agreement. Agreements that in all the cases go beyond the Constitution Statement of the countries involved and morally and economically bound the future of its inhabitants. The strong ones export their surplus, in turn, import raw materials, highly valuable art and cultural goods or acquire land and assets on the weak ones' land, making their way into a slow and pacific takeover, no longer called colonization, invasion or occupation. Money is also lend to the smaller members of the group, ending in a withering economy for the borrowers. There are of course winners on both sides. No, not the people, not the politicians, the big corporations, the ones that had the actual surplus and the need for new markets, the ones wanting cheap over-the-wall materials, the ones longing to place high interest rate credits abroad. These, as you may have thought, are present in every economy, large or small, and prey on everyone, given the opportunity.

The absence of borders allows companies to trade on the rules they can control, on the rules they forge and sustain. Governments are absent from the business table, they have set it free. Now the private game starts. I am free to market in your land but you are also free to do it in mine. We can have an understanding. Can't we? Maybe I am so big that I will just crush you, will take your company and name and will monopolize by-fact the free market of that good. Does this sound familiar? How many supermarket chains do you know in the world? Thousands or a handful? Same question goes for fast food chains, commodities, consumer goods, convenience stores, fuel, communications and shipping, agricultural products brokers and sports leagues just to name them all. Free market? You tell me.

Your personal story as a new corporation would go as follows. In order to succeed, you will have a great idea of an unstoppable product, you will be issued a patent for your product, register your company, install your production line, meet the local requirements, comply with the fire code, check with the ministry of labor, pay all the needed insurance, seek and find the world market and you will be ready to go. Ha!

On that turf of the global economy, once you have the best of products at an affordable price, you lift your head from the desk or laptop, to find yourself facing not a hill to climb, but a wall. You are now finished with the permits and requirements, welcome to the muddy waters of the open free market. After you've met with the chamber of your trade, your local government advisors, the export agency officials, the country of destination imports office, the shipping line and your buyer, you will find out that your product is not as affordable as you expected, and that your competition is setting obstacles faster than you can solve them. Will you sell? Easy, that depends on how competitive you are.

The international price

"...depends on the markets." What a wonderful phrase to explain it all. The ultimate control of the free market is a global price, not *ad-libitum*. The main competition attribute is leveled. Every commodity, for instance, has an index with a behavior depending on the so called law of supply and demand –which, by the way, is one of the series of manipulated trends that the study of economics has stated as law. Of course it cannot rival with the law of gravitation that enables us to place and float in a perfect and accurate orbit our so much needed satellites, or the law of the perfect gas and the three laws of thermodynamics, recently mentioned, that in a precise way make it possible to process agricultural products and chemicals into consumer goods. Economy feels comfortable with naming law something impossible to forecast, but it makes the perfect hiding place for speculation and handling. I guess economy studies suffer from the observer effect where, looking closely into a phenomenon, disturbs it, making the result inaccurate, keen observation blinds the eye-.

With the real science, cause and effect are measured to the millionth or less if needed, their behavior remains the same and fully explained on earth and the heavens. With economy, everything has to be foretold, then the deviations explained, because its science never delivers. I am sure that in your life time you will never witness a perfectly anticipated result in economics. If it were that easy, then governments should be held accountable for all the periods of distress each and every country of the whole world live forever and ever. Is there some sort of actual control? I am intrigued.

Our economy is truly steered by sheer force, by the power of the capital. Different studies and theories arise to explain how it behaves, but trends are only there to justify the underground speculation and management of the markets.

"It was beyond our control," is a statement when a deluge floods a valley, but it is also a justification for every economical backlash, as if we could do nothing about it. Water is eventually controlled, contained and prevented in the future. The same goes for the consequences of powerful earthquakes and new withstanding buildings, only because Civil Engineering has a backup knowledge of laws, real laws. Science uses its knowledge of the natural laws to control outcome.

Lately, Psychology has developed quite accurate psychometric tests. If you have ever been the subject of one, you know that feeling of being dissected. Even human nature is governed by quantifiable laws, but strangely enough, crowd and nation conduct is not, economy is not. Or is it?

 Economic outcome has certain degree of control because it can predict the direction of happenings: what will go up or what will go down –huge guess-, but "...depends on the markets."
Come with me to a flashback of the markets.

Sometime, at a chamber meeting for the producers of a certain commodity, an argument started over one simple fact about whether their only raw material –a recycled one by the way- belonged to a supplier's or a consumer's market and then if they could or not set a price for it. In other words, if the combined purchasing power could determine the value of the materials.

Let me walk away for a moment from the supply and demand trend to state the obvious. If a material is going to be recycled someone has to sort it, package it and store it, sometimes also ship it. Those processes have a cost not related to the market. A recycled material has then a minimum price which, if not paid, then is simply not delivered. The guys on the road picking up cans, PET bottles or recovering glass or cardboard only know what their workday is worth. If you don´t pay it they don't pick it, simple math. Not the commodities fluctuations.

Still, the buyers at the recycling plants believe that hand picking can be a scaled process and that larger volumes will yield lower prices. They do not realize that scale production is only for machines, not humans, and the human machines are basically human, not machine –in every aspect-. On the other reality of recycled materials, they should be able to see that logistics are a big issue. They packed goods and distributed them nationwide, dispersed them nationwide, but expect that through the magic of something called reverse logistics we recover from dumpsters, roads, creeks and dumpsites all of the packaging. They are only failing to see that you have to put at work millions of people to get back what we purchased, without an organized network, without our will to help them, with no retribution involved! What a singular expectation. Of course they will blame on us the environmental damage and insist that we participate thoughtfully to help them accumulate more and more wealth at our expense.

Back to our meeting.

For long, different ways of price controlling had been placed into play: quality specifications and audits, market shares, geographical rights, loyalty bonuses, and futures, but the oligopoly of buyers would not take a stance as to set a price because it was unlawful -how considerate-. On that day, an agreement came into place and the 30 or so competitors decided upon a quality/price relation –no surprise since it is somehow natural-.

"We can't do that, because if we *do* our suppliers will find a way to shift the market. We have to let things be as they are," stated one of the main players by volume.
"Come on. If we stand together they won´t budge," said the largest payer.
"How long can you live without supply? Is your storage full, half full?"
"Beyond the question." Actually meaning 'Is none of your business'.
"Fifteen days? How strong are you? They will brake us."
"No, if we stand together. They will go dry if we do not purchase. They can't last"

The price was fixed and a month later they reconvened, only to find that the prices went up and that the second largest buyer was now the first, having taken over the other's market share. "I told you. You were being naïve," was the only explanation said with the greening face of the winner. Markets are actually handled. A trend is directed. The exact price is never attained, but it is always right for the most powerful participant, in every product and place on earth. Such is life for the competitors of the free market.

The competitive you

You must be a team player. You must be competitive. Come again? Yes, be competitive to climb in life and be a team player to also climb. The concepts seem to be in opposition. Well, they are.

"Hey you, on the back row, is there something you need to tell us? No? OK then, pay attention, listen, if you want to get anywhere in this place."

"If you say nothing during the meeting how do you expect to make progress? Talk, don't just sit there."

You have probably heard the same two sentences from the same person in your organization. Maybe both addressed to you. Do they oppose? Yes. So?

So you must understand the big propaganda and learn when to be competitive -and walk over your teammates- and when to be a humble team player, when to show potential and when to mingle. Of course you don't need this advice. You will be competitive in attitude and actions and will go as far as the ladder goes if you are acquiescent with your superiors. As a result, you will not be popular or wanted among the rest. Perhaps you will be popular and remain with your pairs while somebody –because there are very limited spaces- will climb and get the benefits that go with the position. Nice choices.

What is the real problem here? Think what you would do if you all had the same benefits at any level. Would you climb or not? It is all in the benefits and seldom in the satisfaction of the job itself.

There is a reason why the people upstairs want you to be a team player. They need everybody to stay focused and running smoothly, like a machinery –which is what you are- but at the same time they need some of you to pull the group to higher efforts, to a better performance. They need to throw a competitiveness message. Someone will be promoted because that one made everybody work harder for the same benefit. It is called producing more with less. Be competitive, get the reward.

NINE- GDP / GNP and macro / micro indicators

GDP gross domestic product / GNP gross national product

"The overall value of goods and services generated in a country over a period of time. The total worth of a country's output. It is named Domestic when the measurement is taken within its geographical borders. It is called National when it includes output generated by operations or companies abroad. (this last concept, to measure by flag not by geographic location, often disturbs the data)" (from the 'Basic Economics' Dictionary)

The indicators

Has anyone ever told you not to walk alone at night and, of course, "don't drink the water"? It sounds familiar, it's heard when our citizens travel to those resort places where the western civilization has just started molding their society with our products, our traditions and our jokes. We must enjoy the beach at noon drinking whatever products we have exported there or the brands we have taken over, which are guaranteed to be safe, due to our control.

The situation is quite different when the same thing applies on your own turf, at least regarding your security. Once, at dusk, I was asked by the bus driver while boarding, if I was heading the way the bus was going. I thought so, but I was new in town. It wasn't until the dark night set on and the very dim lights showed an unfamiliar place that I began to think I was going the wrong way. I held my breath, looked around and, long blocks later, I got off the bus at a well-lit corner, where a convenience store and pharmacy proved to be a convenience and a relief all at once. While stepping out, the bus driver turned his look at me, not just followed from the side mirror as they always do, "I knew you were wrong. A bus will come by the other way soon. Hold on. Step inside," as he motioned his finger towards the door of the store.

It wasn´t the first time I had been frightened. It wasn´t the last. I have been mugged or close to being it, in the shining streets at the glamorous quarters of our iconic cities, more than once. I have gotten careful through-out life.

Another time, while visiting one of our most publicized cities, I had the wrong decision of checking into a four star hotel that looked and felt a lot as a two star. The hotel was, however, very well located, next to a square filled with life and amusement. In a particular afternoon, hand in hand, we walked the few blocks that distanced the opera house from our hotel –not much an opera fan, but it was a must visit place, and how can you refuse a recommendation by your travel agent over the desk or the internet, right?-, when at the turn of the street we found ourselves right into a drug dealing sidewalk, just a couple of blocks of highly visible subreptitious activity. I hesitated...

"You don't like what you see?" asked a man sitting on the filthy pavement, his back resting on the wall. I didn't answer. "You ain't got a choice. Keep on walking. It's better. Can't go back." As we followed his advice he added, "Turn down there, by the liquor store. That´s your best chance." We got to the store, bought something –I don't remember what-, looked out the windows and headed out turning, as instructed. We were on time for the opening curtain. I am sure we would have never gotten there in one piece if we had been dressed properly, but recently people not always dress accordingly. Our lack of *etiquette* saved us, but mostly the help of a voice –I never turned to see his face- that guided us through rough waters. Nothing in return, not even my thank you. Heaven sent.

I have, as I said, many other dreadful occasions, but let these two account for an undeniable truth that wealth and progress indicators are wrong. You look at the index at dawn, while preparing for your daily fight at the office and -what do you know-, the world is better than yesterday. A healthy *bourse*, stable consumer prices, the best unemployment rate of all times and our GDP is just booming. Things couldn't be any sweeter. Dirty streets are just from settled dust, not from human beings urinating on them.

What's wrong with GDP? For starters how it is sized.

Picture a car assembly line. There, at the manufacturer plant, input products such as radios, tires, seats, upholstery, wires, paint, shock absorbers, gears, disk brakes, light bulbs, the engine and the gas tank...well the whole car components are bought from third parties that invoice each shipment. In some cases, and truly more than often, those parts come as imports that require the services -also invoiced- of the customs agent as well as cargo insurance -also billed by another company-. The freight is of course charged.
So far, a part that arrives at the production chain has its own value and related services added to it. When the car is finally assembled and sold, its price tag is greater than the value of its parts, which is the amount you and I pay for at the dealer's showroom. This last operation is also economically recorded and summed up as a contribution of the GDP. In this particular example the GDP has been at least doubled: the billed parts plus the vehicle sale.

Let's rename the GDP as GDS: gross domestic sales, by no means product, because the car is *the* product and, viewed from the perspective of wealth, it is only that product that enriched the society where it was produced, distributing along the way some degree of prosperity among the participants of the chain of value just described. The amount of money received by everyone during the process does not add but half of the GDP registered. Is it the only case? Of course not. What's wrong with GDP? For starters, how it is sized.

The GDP has, as an objective, to be the golden indicator of the economy health, as a public wealth index. Considering the GDP as GDS gives an immediate solution to the index validity, however, this denomination change will not reflect the wealth of the country, we end up with the same useless data. Back to square one.

Could we correctly measure the car business contribution on the GDP? Probably yes, but not too easily. We have defined the end product in question: the cars, leaving aside the constituent parts and the services involved up to the final sale –what color did you choose?-, which in theory, have been taken into account already. What about a spare part needed after the vehicle has been sold and used? How many spares should we add or substract from the total production? How many tires, injectors or spark plugs for a vehicle besides the original ones? A part, on its own, can be at some point an end product.

If we wheel away from the car business, we may find a resemblance on other products. In all cases, it looks like the commodities would easily be left out in this approach, since all of them will always become an end product. The same principle applies for the services involved, they will be billed embedded in the end product value, moreover if it is the consumer's end the measurement point.
Some end products are not assembled, but produced directly from raw materials -hence commodities- and some others are farm produce. In both cases the end product approach fits well. Again we have to measure it at the consumer's end, although some goods, before they hit the final user, undergo the change of hands far more than necessary. The price goes up, GDP enlarges, but the value for the society, the wealth, does not.

The question remains as to which considerations should be given for something to qualify as an end product. Let us just have two kinds, consumer and capital goods, both to be measured at the consumer's purchase, everything has been included in the price. Yes, taxes as well. It will be more accurate than the actual GDP –excuse me, the GDS disguised as GDP-.

Let's try another approach.
As far as I know, in capital projects, in order to make a budget for a production line or, for instance, a chemical plant, a profile can be done by adding five general items: main equipment, facilities –buildings and infrastructure-, plant services –steam, compressed air, electricity-, piping and instrumentation, and finally paper work –constitutive formalities and fees, permits, insurance, tariffs and all sorts of auxiliary tasks related costs-. How is this budget truly performed? In some instances, believe it or not, it is calculated to the last bolt and screw at an overwhelming cost just to prepare the budget. In other cases: heuristic values.

If we have an accurate cost of the main equipment, we get, from experience values, the needed infrastructure, the interconnecting piping, the controlling instruments and the energy input. Through experience we know, in percentage, how much to add for each and every case. By the same token, maintenance is calculated for the future, even for a brand new process, all covered by heuristic values. In fact, for a plant recently installed, costs could be examined to find out if some of them by mistake or deliberately, were sawn off or inflated, in exactly the same manner that we would find out and not accept or considered wrong if a vehicle was said to be sold with seven tires and two steering wheels when our common sense, our heuristic value, would dictate four and one respectively.

In brief, this cost calculation starts with the capital goods and the knowledge of the process and ends in heuristic complements for the overall cost.

Learning from the above, another much simpler approach would be to go to the other end, not the product, but backwards through the chain, at the very beginning, to agricultural goods and industry commodities, to solely consider that, as the base of the GDP, applying valid percentages to the rest.

I know, I know, what about a country or region that has, as its chief activity and income, a trading port or it is a tourism destination? Pure services, no goods. Well just that: a service supplier.

To make it clear from this viewpoint, take for instance a corn crop just harvested. The tons produced and the people that will feed will remain the same even after it has been through a sale at an elevator, stored for a while, then resold, trucked to a processing plant, transformed, stored again, sold at a supermarket and eventually consumed. Through-out this process the value changed, but it still has the same capability of feeding as it had in the beginning. It does not feed more people. The product has not multiplied. The steps were needed, no question, but the size and value of all of those steps were already expected from the amount of corn. Let´s just value the cereal, adding a process percentage along the way. The wealth generated is not so badly measured.

A third approach and quite controversial, related to the consumer products, is very simple: only salaries buy products. The wealth of a nation is the amount of wages paid. That is the most realistic indicator for GDP: people´s income.
A question arises when a country produces a surplus that is exported. Somehow the individual earnings will not compare to the amount of the end products. This unmatched figures will be addressed later on, but as an appetizer to the subject, learn that exported products do not add wealth to the country that produced them.

In summary, we have three systems here, from the start of production at its raw materials, at the end of production on the consumer and capital goods, or at the purchasing power. All intimately related to what a nation produces, not to how many times an item was sold or changed hands. Identification of the quantities to add is easier and quite transparent.

In any case, the salaries, the calculation over consumer products alone or agricultural goods and commodities with everything else calculated heuristically will be a lot more accurate than the actual system and will lead to a better knowledge of the prosperity a country is building –the wealth generated- , not this civilization filled with shopping malls, thinking about it as an economy booster or measuring scale.

What else is wrong with GDP? Macro and micro do not match.

"Have you seen our GDP lately? We are rich!" Tell that to everyone, look at their shoes and shirt and, now and then, be ready for a punch or an inquisitive look. Most people will not believe you, merely for you are wrong, even if the GDP looks great.

GDP covers the total economic exchange within a country and someone in your government -surely also in international organizations- assumes that we all profit from those transactions.

For the sake of this argument we must set the meanings of macro and micro.
If we take the world (W) as a whole, then is GWP instead of GDP, its inflation rate – elegantly stated as a consumer price index- becomes a WIR, and job seeking – usually called unemployment rate- would be WUR, just to mention some of the economic indexes by which we follow our monetary health. In that scenario, our GDP would become micro, as there would be as many local indexes as countries there are. Your or my hometown would not be noticeable for either index. The higher we go with the macro indicator, the wider we consider it, the farther it gets from our pocket, from our micro-micro economy. Then, for the purpose of this discussion,

let me define micro as just local, as a township, and leave macro for country sized figures.

Back to our GDP. When we take the GDP *per capita*, most of us will realize that the average income which that figure tells us is not on our checkbook, not in the bill fold, not under the mattress or in the can on the cupboard right beside the stove. We do not make that much. Take out a sheet of paper and draw a one inch line to symbolize your personal assets –which I assume came from your income-, then based on that scale, draw the line for a billionaire...stop! You will require to walk for at least four blocks just for the first billion, if your income is close to the average –take special care if you need to cross the highway-.

GDP does not reflect on its own your living standard or that of your community. GDP *per capita* does not either. It would require another statistical value, called variance, to measure the spread of the money made by you and your fellow citizens, to show how far, you and I are from the average. But you don't need that to know how wealthy you are, how well your family is, how easily you make ends meet or even if you actually undergo that common stress at the end of the month. What bothers most of us is that we are told we are wealthy, by a blunt macro index on paper, which as far as our government´s sight can reach, it means we truly are prosperous. Unfortunately, from the 100th story of a building you can hardly tell any details of the street level. Likewise, the sound of your voice cannot reach that upper level. For short: the gap between the rich and the poor is as wide as the smallest line drawn on paper to the distance between four streets. Your working hour is not as valued as someone else's time. Some are only worth the sprocket they are in the economic machinery, sub-humans within our great civilization.

In some places of the world, within countries, small areas develop local markets, where local GDPs apply to their lives. Those places grow and harvest, breed and operate their *abattoirs* to feed the people, conduct their own banking, struggle to do self-construction and other economic efforts to isolate themselves from the blow of the economy. They are tired of the promises from the few people four blocks away, at the top of the PH, poorly handling our lives.

What is the best GDP average then? Well, a very big one with a very small variance. Is that the country you live in? Congratulations. Is it not? Welcome to the true West-Civ., where micro-micro does not reflect country macro, where the local school cannot be revamped despite the economic growth of the nation.

Something else wrong with GDP? Growth is not always better

We learn that economic growth is a must for an improved living standard. If GDP grows, wealth grows. Really? First we must verify if GDP is adjusted for population growth – immigration included- We need an economy increase at least to equal people growth to keep the same standard, to surpass it if we want to advance. For the moment, let us accept the adjustment is being made and that the magic percentage of three per annum is real growth.

There are, as I said, several ways to boost –really to just barely rise- economic figures, for instance the building of a dam or the enlargement of a merchant port. The economy will look better if a highway is built a thousand miles from your home, although it may mean nothing for you. Now, it is not the gap between those who have more and the less favored, it is if the investment is far or close to your local economy. Growth does not necessarily imply good for all. Maybe in a *ricochet* way some of the benefits will mildly get to you. Don't think twice, the assessment is right, a country has to decide what is best for the country, despite their people. Does it make sense? Good.

Then, we find that a bigger GDP does not mean a better income for you.

In another example, fancy that GDP increases because your government employed more people to perform the same tasks, adding wages, equipment and materials that *positively* impact GDP. Ironically if the boss gets inefficient, GDP grows, your taxes grow, you get a larger GDP *per capita,* but you end up with less in your money clip. Needless to list everything a government can do to increase expenditure against your pocket, *improving* the economy.

There are certainly some government buildings, highways and services that being done in your community will require additional taxes from you. GDP grows again and your personal economy declines.

Another case. An old stadium is demolished and replaced with a shiny new one. More seats, more comfortable, improved lighting, restaurants, ATMs everywhere –same hotdogs fortunately-. All of that implies GDP growth, but no extra coins for you. On the other hand, wealth did not change much for the country, because a good was discarded and only replaced. For practical purposes no net growth as opposed to an increase of the GDP.

As far as a true index for you: trust your pocket, not the GDP. Your pocket is tangible, everything else is make-believe.

We have chosen as an indicator of greatness, money. We have favored it over the arts, over the spirit. The GDP billboard is the perfect outlining feature of our civilization. We compare each of our nations by market power and sales, why wouldn't we then lie on the GDP sizing? If we are to be above the rest, successful, ranked 'second to none', if we are to have the gold medal, then we have to praise to the Gold...May the GOLD be with you...illiterate people.

TEN- Inflation, that relentless ghost

Inflation:

"A condition of continuous price increase of goods and services. Also explained as the drop of the purchasing power of money. It is usually measured as an annual percentage increase of price over a selected set of goods and services" (from the 'You Better Spend Your Money Today' Dictionary)

Inflation rate

At first you have a job and you make savings, and just when you have enough money to buy a car, build a house, buy some land, start your kid's college education fund, you notice that it is not enough. It is never enough. *That* is called inflation, on a soft ride.

I will go on by telling you that, at the heart of our civilization, we have recorded a wide spectrum of inflation rates, as if it were a vestige, but no, it is an extant milestone. Our way of life.
I am sad to bring you into this global, yet self-inflicted reality – actually I'm not-. You see, this western-coined idea involves not only our homeland, it has, within its reach and rules, many second and third world countries striving to be first world players.
If you have not seen inflation rates above 9%, lucky you. Some nations have gone and are going through three and two digits inflation. How in the world can you get that? What fuels inflation? Speculation, the economic carousel.

When a country is in economic trouble, it is common to observe panic overriding people, anxiety about tomorrow and about today, fear that there will be a general shortage of goods and the basic services such as electricity, communications and water. Wizardly, someone else perceives a chance to make a profit by promoting this agitation and simultaneously spike prices. The shortage becomes real powered by speculation...you can get the rest of the picture. If the people in office have sufficient support and strength, it can be prevented, but usually this is not the case. This is just one in a hundred stories about inflation in extreme cases.

Perhaps we regard as natural for prices to climb when the production costs go up. This is in fact true for increments on energy, supplies and salaries. So, don't be surprised that you will not get a pay raise because it boosts inflation.

Inflation is a stubborn boy with its mild behavior exceptions, oil, for instance.
Oil prices go up and everything goes up. Oil prices go down and...oil prices go down. Get it? No? OK, let me be more specific.
Oil prices go up and gasoline prices go up. Oil prices go down and gasoline prices go down, but never to the historic lows. For some reason the gallon price remains high but, since it floats, it makes you feel that you are not being cheated. Why isn't this the behavior of the rest of the goods? Why everything else is permanently flying higher and higher?

Place in your mind for a moment an industry. Their expenses are divided in at least, purchase, production, maintenance, transport, storage and sales –in some cases research and development-. In every step we have supplies, energy and wages. There is a so called cost structure, where you can easily explain what should be the end price when a cost item varies. If energy prices go up 5%, it does not mean that the product will need to go up 5%. You need to calculate that from the structure. What sort of inflation will a 20% increase in salary return? You tell me.

What is inflation's purpose then, if any? Easy, to protect the corporations' profit, the owner's income if you may see it that way. A cost increase results in a price increase to adjust the gain, but profit must not remain the same, because the inflation has caused it to reduce its value, prices must be higher that the balance. You don't agree. Well, that's how it works.

Now, in the first place, why do prices go up? Supply and demand? No, plain speculation. Look at the following paradox.
After the industrial revolution, chain production became the rule. The world could finally produce something with a high output at a low cost. It had said 'good bye' to the artisan, *le maître de l'atelier* was gone for good. A pair of shoes, a shirt – a watch at a time-, could be afforded by anyone. Same goes now for a car and every conceivable good. Does it really?
As I understand, technology –the know-how-, has made the continuous processes more efficient every decade. The so called scale economy is riding the same coach, producing more at a lower cost. What is wrong then? With better production methods, improved research, upgraded logistics for storage and transportation, etc., how can we account for higher prices? We can. It is logical, 'the lower the cost, the higher the profit' or, 'the higher the price, the higher the profit', period.

There are, certainly, the unobjectionable explanations. 'Our globalized world is complex.' -You can never beat that one-. 'Markets are changing, evolving.' –Unpredictable, for sure-. 'The unsteady situation in that particular region of the globe, makes things uncertain, unsafe for business.' –Clear as spring water-. Yes, yes, yes, we have been enlightened.

Inflation is meant to be

Just to end the note on GDP. You probably thought that GDP must also be adjusted to cover for inflation. Again, let´s assume it does, but be aware that GDP is simply manipulated by inflation, because inflation is, above all, the equivalent of the immunodeficiency syndrome for economy, the most powerful eraser of it, the most vindictive tool ever invented to wipe out any stable society.

You are sort of lost? Inflation a tool? 'Above all', inflation is a principle of our civilization? Obviously there is a lot to say about it.

At the beginning there was no money and no inflation. No matter how many words and reasoning are placed to the understanding of inflation –believe me, pages and pages have been written about it-, its origin dates back to that of money and to that of interest rates. I will not tire you talking about the balance between the value of goods and the amount of money, but listen for a moment. Needless to say that if you print more money and still have the same quantity of goods, either the goods will be revaluated to balance the amount of money –same as saying the money will buy less-, or the extra amount of money will turn worthless, because at a permanent, unchanged, price it would have no goods to buy. Well, having said that, here is a way to print money relentlessly: the so called interest rate. Inflation may be influenced by the circulating amount of money –never to the minus rate, strangely-, but you can bet that interest rate will always produce inflation, because it will always increase the amount of money. Who is really burdened by interest rates and who is not? If you are an investor, keep in mind that, at its lowest, interest rates will match the inflation figure, your investment will have no loss or gain. At its peak, you will make money. Yes you will actually be manufacturing or making money –as you say-, printing money or, in today's terms, electronically adding money. If you have mega, giga or tera, amounts of it, inflation is on your side. On the contrary, if you have a weekly salary that lasts only your week, a biweekly one that gets you through half the month or a monthly payment that is dried at day one or two of the next period, then you are doomed, and inflation, disregarding its rate, depletes your wealth.

Inflation seems not to be a pillar of our civilization, but it is. It helps sustain the needed class differences, to tackle upcoming undesirable humans, to keep them in permanent check. The less advanced, the less developed, a country is, the higher rates can be upheld. It is the control tool. We remain on top.

Of course we can induce inflation an also "make money" by merely raising prices, but just tell me how would it look if only my product became more expensive? Fingers would be pointed at me. If a couple of other entrepreneurs did the same those forefingers would still point at us. Thus, we develop a ghost, something outside our control, beyond our powers, that cripples everyone, even my business, something that no one can stop or dodge: we create inflation. No more fingers, no more accusations. We are all victims of the phantom: inflation. Consequently we need a team of dedicated people to help us understand it and predict it. We suffer not being able to foresee. We record the past but no math enables us to foretell. What a pity. The solution dawns on us: let's increase the value of our money, let's apply interest rates. We are saved. The effect becomes the cause and vice versa. We are clever.

Can you envision a world without inflation? Without interest rates, where budgets would only consider sales and purchases at fixed prices? A whole set of schools and specialties in economics would be without purpose. All those equations and stats to predict the unpredictable would lose its sparkle. From the shadows of knowledge would arise the untangled simplicity of the 'constant value'. You may think: "that can't be." I say: "we don't want it to be," because for the few in control of the many, it is the perfect tool. No one to blame, at the marrow of economy.

In the light of this, should money be banned? No, certainly not. We need a practical way of trade, of exchange, with tokens or electronic zeroes and ones. We need a value standard. We need money. The devious concept is that money grows on its own at a fixed or variable rate. If saleswoman Mrs. Right delivers a product to buy another product from salesman Mr. Left, there must be an equivalence between the two products so that, at any time, Mrs. Right must sell the same amount to buy also the equivalent amount. Suddenly money comes in for the trade and, before you notice it, takes life on its own and the equivalence is lost, because money grew due to something called interest rates, disguised as inflation. The trade is off.

Maybe I should understand that money is invested. It is not seating and growing. It is invested, thus grows. The peculiar thing about it is that the rates never lose. The investment always yields. The overall balance always draws profit. Money becomes more money and, along, inflation continuously rises.

Inflation is the constant of our times. It defines our western world. It is rooted in our lives and in everything we do. It is another trade mark, perhaps *the* trade mark.

Finally, just for my enjoyment I ask, "Do you earn money or rather make money? Do you work for it or wait for it?

ELEVEN- The financial system

Finance:

"Basically, the management of money. Word originated in the 15th century meaning an end to a debt. The money administration is nowadays essentially connected to banking, investment and credit" (from the 'Who Owns Your Assets?' Dictionary)

Money and interest rates. Is there a body devoted to it? Yes there is: the financial system. Let´s scan its fibers.

Currency and trade

When we abandoned the small town economy and distances were no longer measured in miles but in hours or minutes, our world had already changed. Certainly the industrial revolutions shaped our world. A higher productivity, a quality standard and a lower cost, placed the production of our consumer goods and capital products in the hands of industrial operations, away from the highly qualified craftsmen, whom, on a very small scale, survive to deliver top class objects at much greater values, where a uniqueness attribute and numbered articles become the pride for ownership.
Even in the dirt fields, the production of food had a renewed technology, along with the same features as the chain production, except for the chain itself.
Curiously, none of the above improved trade, for trade is time-dependent and has no direct relation to productivity or the other characteristics just mentioned. I know, some of you disagree.

Trade may be desirable for a certain product –all of them you would say-, but trade is only possible if the distances are short enough for it. Suez and Panama are very clear examples of this. The two channels improved trade without merely touching quality, efficiency or even price. Trade is time-dependent. OK now?

On a smaller landscape the same thing can happen. There are places in the world where large and long mountain ranges split lands and separate cities and countries that, although neighbors, have very little trade. The same case applies for oceans, rivers, lakes, bays, jungles, marshes or any other geographical accident. I am sure you can think of an example very near your home for any of these.

On those cases you thought about, you will find that trade was made possible by a bridge, a barge, a railroad or a highway, not by productivity and competitiveness.

We developed means of transportation that have also been upgraded throughout time, as one of our most precious assets since the invention of the wheel. At the early stages of high distance trade, the effort to shorten time was, as it is today, the real objective. We have maritime, land and air vehicles, not always at affordable prices but just available for trade.

Let me fall into an already referred subject dealing with trade: The free trade agreements. The only possible ones are not only those that have a geographical area in common, but those that within that area have no additional geo-accidents. So your government can promote and sign hundreds of agreements –more likely of good intent between countries-, but only those that will work and generate flow are where the flow is possible. As evident as this is, should it be to you that there is no world market, you can only compete on the block, the nearby area where you can reach, thus sell. What a revelation!
Here it is for you a new law of economics, just as clever as all the other we know and just as obvious and useless: "trade is in

indirect proportion to time and in direct proportion to unit delivery capacity". Maybe I read it somewhere, I just don't remember where.

You are still reluctant to the idea of remoteness as a deterrent. Please follow me through a simple exercise.
Place yourself as a giant on top of a map comprising five countries, one at the center and four at its perimeter. Now, place yourself in the middle country, invite your fellow giants, representing the other four, to trade. Who has the easiest trade? Run the example with three countries in a row, again with you in the mid one, do the opposite sides trade as much? You are probably an obstacle, wouldn´t you say? Distance is of no importance, right? –Pass me the salt, please-.

I know a peculiar case where two competitors, of the now very common recycled commodities, despite biting each other for the market of their end products, would team up along the long border dividing their countries -and their factories as well- to buy from the other and import the scrap they used as raw materials, one heading north, the other south bound as an exchange, in order not to recover and then ship on either side of their 1200 miles of route. Then, the one in the west end would collect on the south to be processed a few miles to the north. The other one on the east side would gather on the north and deliver for production in the south. All this exchange at face value, pound per pound – of weight that is-. A true trade in the very times of the kingdom of money.

There are in the same recycling industry other cases of pure trade. When ships cross the oceans to deliver products –what did I just say about distant markets? I must really make up my mind-, on their way back there is the need to ballast to control buoyancy. It is done with water if no other weight available. How about coming back with some, easy to handle, bales of materials to recycle? Yes, there is a money transaction included, but is not a shipment order, just an exchange of favors, freight for counterweight. Money is the least involved.

For many of you all of this is not new. It is even boring, sorry. It gets worse now that we move into money.

I said it myself: currency is needed. In the case of trade, it is the second indispensable element. The longer the distance the greater the need for money. Simple coinage at first on the incipient exchange, it has travelled far. It is unthinkable to perform exchange of goods without a reference value, e.g. money. Instead of exchanging goods you could, since then, buy and sell through the equivalent. Money represented –still does- all the goods, the exchange became not of goods to goods but goods to money.

Money was a great invention. It has come a long way from seeds and tablets, through forged coins and metals, to the electronic money that today extends to broader benefits, since it shortens time for the exchange and locks the operations. Whereas our high tech vehicles still take a long time to supply, the almost lighting speed of credit assures the transactions. Don't hate money –some of you do, I know-, do not love money either –some of you do, I know-, think of it as a tool. Its corruption is not a birth mark, it came later.

The money managers

Today, in our modern world, there are the money keepers, banks, trusts and the biggest scam of all: the *bourse*.

The trusts hold money and other assets in behalf of the beneficiaries, with locks and containment rules that make them the best example of money handling in a responsible way. Its qualities do not reach the rest of the money handlers. The money is truly invested in productive activities, the profits are shared or not if none.

Let me continue –as if I gave you a choice- with the stock market. Companies are worth three things: their physical assets –land, buildings, machinery, equipment, vehicles and up to the last clip and staple- the money in their accounts –

please consider all the cash, debts, loans, everything into just accounts- and their market. Of course its inventories of products and raw materials – if a manufacturer-, but it is useless to further complicate things, as I will later on explain. The value is written on paper and divided into shares, just as you can divide lottery tickets in some places, similar to the way we scribbled our child money from a blank page and sort of carefully cut out eight bank notes. In a justified way, if any of this companies augments those assets, the value rises and your torn ticket is more valuable. There is no argument about the first two –physical assets and bank accounts- but how about the market?

Market mainly means sales and thus future earnings for your share, but momentarily nothing for certain. However, humans speculate about the near and mid-term profits which, if favorable, will cause a rise on the value of your green or brown certificate, although no real value is sustained. Suddenly another trend, another rumor, will come and the value will collapse even below your other assets sum. You will have on your hands some fancy paper clippings.

So, no matter the real worth of your company –it is yours in a way- you and the enterprise are subject to gossip, to sensational news, a virus outbreak, a poisonous comment, a natural catastrophe, well…it can even be blamed for a presidential coup somewhere in the world, you can be praised or hated and your investment responds along those lines. It is so subjective that you can also triple your gains overnight and lose everything by noon –my advice, sell at breakfast-.

During the process, shares change hands and money flows. The corruptive part about it is that value is being created out of the blue –unsustained, uncontrolled-, fortunately, for most of us, the real loser is the individual that bought a bright future that never came, giving away his money to someone else in exchange for the ownership of a broken company.

There are in many cases real possibilities of growth in a company, but they are as limited as the market itself, whereas hearsay has no boundaries. Nevertheless, occasionally the sudden or slow fall of a company –or its slow rise- can truly be predicted, because a new technology sat in, a new law forbade some of its components, a workers strike froze the company, a new development offered new markets, a military invasion did as well or a competitor ran out of business, just to mention a few. The problem is when proportions get out of hand and, rumor has it, they do. They are ignited to happen. We, the mortals on the ground, away from the 45th floor, more than often in an indirect way, are bound to lose, because those speculations can cause the job market to stir, the interest rates to shift. It can be made on purpose, explained by complex theories with wording hard to be understood or expert speeches that leave two words in our mind: oh my!

The money managers in this case have earnings in every sale, they never lose. They profit from the exchange, depriving one side and enriching the other. At the same time they nurture price changes and interest rate evolvement.

That part of the game is beyond our hands and comprehension –if the players, the gamblers can't do it, why should we?-, but the banking side seems to be within our grasp. Yes, it is easier to understand.

The money managers have banks. They safeguard our money and invest, including the stock market unquestionably. They also foretell results by applying well calculated loans to companies, certainly based on the short time return on investment outcomes. Our money is lent at rates superior to the ones we get, our savings are being protected. Since interest rates have no real control in most of the countries, the transactions are market controlled. The banking market controls itself, sets the rules for the game.

I've already profiled that principle –common knowledge- about money printing becoming a cause of inflation. I also mentioned that is just what happens when you print electronic money through that simple tool called the interest rate. Constantly, ceaselessly, banks increase the amount of money in circulation with that quantity placed into their electronic servers. The exchange of money for goods is, at that point, corrupted, because goods have an added cost without added value –e.g. your mortgage will raise the cost of your house but will not make its worth move a notch up-. That added cost is profit for the bank and inflation for you. The bank is not charging for a service provided, it is, in a percentile fashion, chewing your assets, putting a hand in your pocket, or the pocket of a country in precisely the same manner. The bank is literarily making money.

Let's get into a small operation within a bank. A corporation requires money for a project, expecting to start yielding profits in five years –i.e. having paid the loan in five years or a 20% yearly profit on the capital invested-. The bank receives money from you and others that will be placed on that project. The maximum payable rate that it could apply on its corporate customer is to equal the profits at 20%, but the company would be only working for the banks amusement, pay the interest, none of the principal and gain nothing ever. If the bank charged a 10% rate, the corporation would pay the principal in ten years and it would start having profits by then. If the bank only charged 5% then in 6.66 years the deal would take place. In any case, the interest rate agreed upon would only be a cost, the price of money. But we are moving into unknown territory, no scouts have been sent there. A bank wouldn't charge that low just as much as a company would not accept a longer payback period. The bank, actually, will also have a surcharge on something called risk. The risk of not getting paid, because the deal could go wrong, because the project could go down the drain.

What truly happens is that the bank, for starters, keeps –veiled or not- the ownership of the good until paid for –just like it does on your house-, then it requires another guaranty of the same amount, a collateral good, to end up charging the risk, then 5% is out of the question. What then? In order to comply, the company makes a simple move, mainly to shorten the payback period. How? Easy: higher prices, bigger profits. In this perverse and indirect way interest rates impact inflation. Just as in the first case the intermediary makes profits, you earn a little with your deposit at the bank, the corporation earns money and you...you pay the price –of the product that is-. The bank is a real money maker, not just a money handler.

Inter-nation bank operations

Not happy enough to deflate our savings, banks get into an international trade of their own: money lending to states, to countries.

Countries have central banks to regulate their currency and are the real money makers, the money printers. They coexist in an unorthodox and colliding way with the other banks, the private ones, because central banks are devoted to stabilize the economy and promote development, whereas the private sector just to make profit. Believe me these goals do not match, they oppose each other.

More than often, countries –especially those underdeveloped-, require funds for several purposes, such as infrastructure, education, research or even for profitable projects to, for instance, process raw materials into commodities for the world market. Also, it is very common for them not to have the needed funds and to apply for loans. The money managers have provided a rule of "no money printing" to finance the projects, since it is inflationary. Is it?

A country could easily print money to get things rolling within the country and, even better, to produce within the country the goods needed for the project. That would boost development, but would not promote sales in the form of exports from the more powerful countries, where the money managers reside, here, in our society. The prohibition to print money seems a business based one, not an economical one. When the project is done and the operation is ongoing, the country instead of using the profits could simply burn the loan, destroy the bank notes -erase the money it printed-. At its payback period no money would have been added to the market and no interest rate would have been paid. Printing money would have not caused inflation, on the contrary a loan would have. It is all about responsible management, not about economic rules from the world's financial system.

It makes you wonder if such a strategic asset as money should be allowed to be in the hands of individuals or if it should be handled by the state for the benefit of its people. I know, you must think that governments are corrupt. I think that, since the same materials that compose governments also make up the private systems, maybe our risk of corrupted financial systems is the same. Both have and share one quality: they are in power. No, you are not.

Make it complex

If you are the financial system and you want to make your home refractory to outsiders, you must be clever enough to make things really complex, highly cumbersome, by adding detail to its operation and underlying principles. No one should be able to understand anything. Every explanation must have its counter-explanation. Every trend should be partially explained with a huge set of conditions to be met. The result is to develop pages and pages on the economic subject that will deviate the attention from your system and will end up grading it as indispensable. Can you grasp a world without the financial system? Some small, educated, modern, productive regions, developing regional markets and economies believe so. They produce, distribute and consume local. They use money but not the traditional financial system.

Thousands of books have written in the past century to explain every aspect of the economic system of the western civilization. Books to predict the outcome of strategies. Books to explain unemployment, energy crisis, industrial recession, housing boom, poverty, inflation, the markets, price changes, growth. Books based on the complexities of the system, based on the fuzzy trail that has been described to be the solid foundation, but that are only crispy fallen leaves on the dirt path never to be seen underneath. We stumble with the rocks we don't see, and crush the leaves into a powder of protection for the simple truth, the simple power of the system: to confuse and hide.

The study of economics is surrounded by math, based on it. Thick volumes with explanatory theories backed up by equations of transitory states such as our present, where the dynamics of growth, competition and trade are quantified and projected. Asymptote graphs showing the inflexion points that determine the best moment in time or the perfect gap to invest, the point of lowest risk, of maximum gain. They statistically view and study ours and other societies, pinpointing changes. It is very, very complex, debates continue without end to explain our today. They reach the goal of isolation. They are not clear, but are untouchable. They are complex beyond reason.

The currencies and their equities

Nations have their own currency, establishing parities between them. What a problem!

Think of any given product that to be produced uses up several raw materials, involving agriculture, industry and distribution services. Imagine now that we set up a price in every currency. At that moment we would have a parity for every coin considered. The more complex the product, the better for this comparison. But now, ponder that a central bank somewhere decides to print money, the parity would be offset with that currency. How do you control that? Anyone at ease can change the value. If at the same time in every country the other banks, the private ones, decide freely on their interest rates, then the actual value of a currency resides in too many hands.

Before not solving that problem, let's be for a moment in a country that needs to promote growth and employment, choosing to boost productivity as a solution. Simple enough, it looks at the foreign market and decides to sell cheaper to improve exports, devaluates its currency so others can buy more product for the same amount of foreign currencies. This is one of the many manipulations that the central banks and the diverse financial systems can force upon the economy. A universal currency is needed? A world bank at the world's service? Would you trust that? Would it become, instead, the renewed control machinery of the money makers? Would it simply turn into a world chamber or association of some sort for our beloved money handlers? What? You are telling me that it is already in place and doing precisely just that? Gosh! How many questions so bluntly answered, except for one, do you trust that?

Back to our currencies problem.
We could follow the price and parity of our equivalence product, but how do you control someone from printing wealth to buy more of that product with their overloaded currency? Maybe through the financial system, right? And who controls that system? The central banks? No, in its place, the money makers controlling their counterparts. If they team up you and I are lost. Guess what, we are.

Finally, our main problem rests the -very simple- same, the self-reproduction of money.

GDP and the financial system

These money managers have made us believe that they are needed more than energy, more than production, more than oxygen itself. They are at the core of every move in the world, from the armament escalation to the purchase of bananas at the supermarket. The planetary exploration, the new technologies, the study of subatomic particles is only possible because of them –so they claim-. Their contribution to world is called a credit, something so valuable –they claim as well- that it is also included in the GDP.

TWELVE- Taxes and *the* government

Tax:

"A money payment enforced by governments on their citizens or companies, as a percentage of their income, their assets or the value of the economic transactions. These imposed contributions are redistributed as services and infrastructure for the public benefit" (from the 'There is a Pie Slice Missing' Dictionary)

Government

"The appointed people in charge of a country. The group planning, organizing, legislating, executing, directing and controlling the purpose of a country" (from the 'You Were Born Here' Dictionary)

The indivisibility of taxes and government

We have taxes because we have a government, they are one and only. The very moment you create one, the other one is born. That is also true in our Western Domain.
We have a marked aversion for governments and taxes - rather for authority and income cuts-. Certainly, in feudal times, imposts to the crown or lords were probably out of proportion, as if the rulers were just for the take, perhaps they were.
We know today that self-appointed administrations are an outdated concept, the decision power is now in the hands of the people for the good of the people. It is no longer in the hands of a few. Why that face? I am wrong?
Regardless of our dislike for governments, we must accept the fact that we need a performing body, an organized assembly with its own set of rules, infrastructure and all the other material means, to deliver community services -for short, a

government-. Face it, you need a referee, at least, to avoid anarchy, but...taxes?

Taxes, what for?

"Do we need taxes?" Was the question raised one day by our teacher in high-school, right after all the chairs and tables had been laid to the sides of the room as to allow for a possible speaker to be in the middle, or probably just so that no one had to turn the head around to look at the classmate talking. The place was exactly the same way we set it to have a discussion, on another day for another question: "Do we have freedom?" We all enjoyed, I guess, this amphitheater distribution of the classroom, seated on the tables instead of the chairs. The session was to be amusing.

"Do we need taxes?" He asked, as the last one of the tables had been set screeching, leaving a trace on the floor, for the enjoyment of the janitor.

After a debate of fifteen minutes by a very few willing to talk, our teacher had to intervene, "I am not asking if you or your parents like taxes," and after a pause, "It's very simple, do we need them? Just think and give the class a reasonable opinion. Don't tell us what you hear at home! Tell everyone *here* what you think!" I quickly gathered that the complaints I heard at home and on the TV were just nonsense.
I recall understanding that yes, taxes are needed.

We have a society's supra-structure that carries out tasks for the community. It makes studies of the society, develops long and medium term plans, decides and executes the enlargement and improvement of the nation's infrastructure, provides various services throughout the territory, promotes union, assures peacekeeping and order, upholds and spreads our culture –believes, aspirations, behavior paths, traditions and language, just to mention some of it-, gives guidance and, at last, regulates our daily motion and activities as one self-identified pack. For that, it needs income to operate. Taxes are needed.

On the opposing side, some people think about the things we never use, that our taxes pay for, as that highway on the other side of the country, the remodeled House of Representatives, the X's Syndrome Hospital, an obelisk or monument on the street lawn, the new Science Museum, the Bureau of Wildlife Stats, the renewed snowmobile course or the repair of the mountain railroad, just as examples. Some then believe that taxes should apply on demand, that we should only be charged for the services received at the needed moment, but the spot tax –like the name?-, requires the government body to be ready at all times, on stand-by mode, and asks for a complex payment calculation.

In various sports, there are players that are on the field for brief moments, for a swing, a single play, the last ten minutes of the match. They are play-makers. A season's team effort rests on their shoulders at times. Should their payment be according to the time performed or to their availability for the team? They are present and ready every minute of the games, throughout the tournament.
Likewise, professionals stand ready to provide an advice or service. Most of them only charge for the 'borrowed time' at an exorbitant rate –we believe-, maybe to account for the inactivity periods. Availability has a cost.

I must agree that tax collection is all but simple. Our government is eager to cash in as much as possible, resulting in awkward rules that only accountants comprehend. It certainly does not help. Their lack of imagination causes our intolerant mood towards taxes.
I also understand the complexity of providing a service that not all people use, but that at some point they could require. Somehow there is a mix between fixed and some variable costs. You actually deliver an amount to cover the continuous cost –the availability- to your dear taxman, but once in a while, when you get a hold on specific services, you cover a

variable cost, such as a fee for your driver's license or the entrance to a national park. Is it really that bad?

Government works no doubt, in our civilization, for the common good, despite our selfishness and that of the appointed officials who govern us. It is not a perfect system to handle our group, but it works. It fulfills its goal. Statistically has a much higher grade than we award it. Whatever your opinion, you must conceive that it cannot perform *pro bono*.

Hand it to the private enterprises

Yes, let's go private. We don't need the load of that slow moving, heavy and large government. Make it lean. The government on a diet, really?
To me it sounds chaotic. We better think it over, carefully. Come along to review if there aren't a few things that are so fundamental, so risky, that we should have a government in control of them.

Our society has had in the far and recent past, and has ahead, a very long debate about what economic and social activities are meant to be state-controlled and operated, and which ones by the citizens, what deserves the public hands and eyes, and what else could go to the private black-box. In some cases, nations believe that the strategic should be public, the rest private. However a question pops-up, what is strategic?
Should energy be considered strategic -oil, natural gas, electricity and geothermic power-? How about communications –telephone, TV, radio, the internet, railroads, roads, airports and maritime ports with its courses and routes-? Think about education, should it be regarded as strategic? Law drafting as well? Fresh water systems from the aquifer or lake and right to your kitchen faucet, strategic? Is food production strategic or just a good, taken for granted? Are consumer goods in that category? Should I include mining?

Let me throw in the militia, insurance and health care. All for you to ponder.

Please, if you can, put aside the social, economic and political dogmas that surround your life -for one that 'governments are corrupt and inefficient', as if privately owned enterprises were spotless and on the verge of sanctity, for another that 'competition is better for all'-. Put aside everything and think what is reasonable, just like our wise teacher stated. You can't?

Oh! There is someone on the third row that has a point. "Come again ma'am?"
"I said that we can't have the military in private hands."
"How come?"
"Isn't it obvious? They're us. They're our great country. Private?"

'I'm with her' I say. We want the military to be committed with the nation. To be loyal. To help us to be autonomous. To protect our sovereignty. To not turn against us ever. Oh my! I just realized that it is what we would expect from all the other bodies dealing with water, energy, minerals, food...We would expect national commitment.
At least, we would want to have regulations for each activity in our nation that would, first of all, care for those at home, as a household does.
Will a private corporation, whose first commitment is with its shareholders, perform the job? Keep in mind that their target is called money-making, not service-providing, thus, strategic tasks –nation's fundamental activities- should be performed by the government or at least regulated by it.

If you are those who think that all the activities –law making comprised-, can and should be done by the private citizens, well...welcome to the land without government, the land without order, the land where the better fit will dine on the others. Yes, you move up front, you're next.

The size of your tax

Our nations, inside the walls of the western civilization, have different viewpoints as to what should be controlled by the government and what shall remain market-controlled. Some have state-owned electrical power plants and distribution. Some have medical staff and institutions on their payroll. Some have railroads. Most regard education as something to be done by the state but allow for private interference. Some monopolize water. All monopolize law drafting and upholding.

We do not seem to fully agree on what to do and what not to. In any case, if not fully, the ministries in every nation embrace all of the activities, so that at least the government has certain control over them to protect you. This protection and care is enforced whether the operator is the government itself or a private organization.

The size of your tax depends on the size of the activities of the government. If it is truly inefficient as you think, then the tax grows. There is no government other than the tax-taking one, it is out of the subject to discuss its behavior in this matter, because basically it is *always* going to have capital expenditure, as well as continuous costs, which brings me to the next question, do you think you are getting a better deal or will get a better deal if all the public services and economic activities were privately executed? Girl! This is a tough one – regretfully, nowadays I can't say, 'boy! This is a tough one'-.

How much do you think it costs to draw a cubic foot of water from a water-table and bring it to your bathroom? Measure the distance, the depth, the pipe diameter, the terrain it traverses, the pump, the electricity consumed, the power lines. Not endless, but quite a few items to consider. All of that, plus the operators and the administration above them, bring about the cost of your cubic foot. It doesn't matter who operates the distribution system, the cost at equivalent efficiency of work and overhead, turns out to be the same, but –yes, there is a 'but'- if it is ran by your government it will not have an added profit cost. So, in the best of cases, you will pay more if it is privately owned, due to something called the entrepreneurial greed.

It is useless to argue whether a monopoly, an oligopoly or the *true* free market will bring a better result than a committed-to-the-nation operation. As for the basic cost of your service, it will be the same in all cases, paid via taxes or directly to the *entrepreneur*. That is how things truly work in economy. You cannot pay below the cost, although you can always pay above in our society.

How about subsidies? You may wonder. We all pay them via taxation, but it appears they are planned and implemented for the common good.

No more water talk, risk to examine with me the price of insurance, your actual insurance fees. Take away the profit from the insurance company and tell me what's left. Would that fee go down if it were state-owned at a 100% population coverage? If you are an actuary, please do the math –leave aside your dogma hat and please do the math-.

Now, conceive a national electrical grid, with its related costs. Would your bill be lower or higher?

I get it, you want toll roads and bridges, from the local, past your regional and up to your national paved strips. Perhaps you long for private cemeteries and hate municipal town markets, as much as you dislike public piers and harbors.

Is it that you want to have access only to private elementary, high schools and universities?

All of it for a small supplementary cost called the shareholders profit. At the end, of course, private police and private judges, whom, on the free elastic market, would charge you according to the size and opportunity of the case and would grant justice sized to your wallet.

You can easily notice that there is more than meets the eye. It is a mixture of economic and moral issues –social and freedom issues some democracy fanatics would argue-.

Wouldn´t you say that for many of these public needs the government is more reliable? I believe it is much more trust worthy, it does protect you from the predators.

Stop complaining about the size of your tax. Our government is actually charging for a service direct cost and adding an overhead. It is there where we shall act. Make them deliver as promised, protect you the most possible, engage in all the critical, strategic, activities. Forget the entrepreneurship propaganda and ask, is your government falling short of the required mark? Demand compliance.

THIRTEEN- Surveillance

Surveillance:

"To closely watch, oversee and track movements or actions of something or someone for control purposes" (from the 'Lab Rats are Watching Back' Dictionary)

We need a government but...

No question we want and need protection, education, a law abiding life, health and wealth. The protection part however, has opened the door to a surveillance abuse where we have lost our privacy, where each move is watched or at least recorded for further use.

Our lives have never been without watch, but the new data acquisition and handling capabilities have increased the scrutiny and detail. 'Who', 'when', 'where', 'how' and 'what' are quite evident on the records. 'Smile, you are on camera.' 'You are being watched for your safety' are only two of several ways –when informed- about the close observation of which we are the target. 'Why' remains always to be established by the watcher. It has made it easier to be followed, to be stalked, to be harassed by the government, sometimes in the electronic network of the mindless server, occasionally in the eye of another human. In the first case anonymity and privacy more or less remains intact. In the second one, we are completely exposed.

Ever since the occurrence of the law enforcement bodies, the people were watched and controlled, since the purpose of following our moves has always been to restrict our lives to the approved code. It is not till our modern times that those suppressing corps have started to become a protection and aid for the community. We are progressing, but don't party just yet.

We are sold the idea that by watching everyone we are going to be secure, as the result of a total coverage. However, is not yet total and we, the citizens of the first world, are more closely recorded than any other people in the rest of the world. The tapes will show when someone outside the nest comes into the picture or someone from the nest behaves awkwardly, then our society will act through its enforcers to restore peace and quiet even before trouble happens.

We get used to being watched. We get used to losing our independence and freedom.

No denial there is about the fact that, some way or another, we are a target. We earned that risk by imposing ourselves on other societies and preying on them. In some instances, because of our insane preventive actions abroad, since we have gotten over our head the right to rule and conform the world to our liking and creed.

We increased that potential by our abusive foreign policies, in exactly the same manner our internal policies have upset the balance of our communities, creating the dangerous poverty zones in our cities, where people dwell hoping for the chance that will change their lives forever. Meanwhile, the cat eyes survey the land ready to jump on the intruding mice or the flying trespasser.

Becoming paranoid

Once you are amid cameras, mikes and internet automatic filing servers, you may as well become paranoid. You can possibly begin to think that something you said or wrote will be your perdition. Why can others feel at ease with all of this? There are films, books, radio and TV shows that stress how fragile we are against the total power of data gathering that the system has. Every purchase, every door crossed, every telephone call, all internet mail, each picture uploaded to the cloud —as if the clouds were an ethereal place where we could hide our dearest dreams-, the short spoken message we sent to the group of friends, the clip we opened from a colleague, all of it, binds our acts stronger than the most powerful glue.

Don't worry. It is just one of the faces of our times. Your best way about it is to accept it and live in normality. The more ordinary you are, the less trouble you mean for the system. It upsets you? Well, get over it. It will not go away. Even mistrusted, it is for the good of all and only against those who defy your way of life, who threaten your limited freedom. Get it?

The corporate act

The vigilance is not only governmental. It is seriously done at the inside of companies, at its headquarters, branch offices and factories or warehouses. Union's disapproval met endorsed government reasons, such as safety, in favor of taping the operation. How in the world could we know for certain how, when, etc… an accident had taken place, if not for the help of our tireless camera?

A landslide of reasons came after that: the need to protect the facilities and the process from possible sabotage, the convenience of catching the instance and circumstances surrounding that equipment failure, the time when the machine started to hum in a very regular, very productive way. Now 'taking the picture' of the best operating condition became a reality. How could you not accept being watched?

Naturally, every incident could be reviewed, over and over again, by the tape holders. Unwanted happenings could be tampered with. The impartial witness could be silenced or freed to give testimony. A very convenient tool for the management –as any other to be used for good or bad, but convenient-.

Corporations found what they later passed unto public life. They discovered the legally bound way to control the people: movement inside the factory; regular or casual meetings; lunch time conversations; who meets who; when it happens; all of it to be filed in case of need, in case of insubordination.

"You musn't stay long here," a maintenance supervisor friendly advised us.
"Why?" I asked, a little puzzled by the way he approached us, walking steady, instead of slowing down.
"You're being watched. You've been here almost twenty minutes. Doing what?" He said while he brushed passed the three of us.
"Where? How?" I asked.
"We installed new cameras here last Saturday. Don't look up," he said, eyes on the floor ahead of him, always walking.
"We're going over the compressor break down..." I started to shout to the man rapidly distancing from us.

Yes, we were questioned later that day about our inaction during that exchange of ideas on our improvised meeting room in the middle of the plant. Corporations hire you to act, to do, to prove yourself useful, not to idle over anything.

I wonder how often I have done things that resemble other than that actually done. I wonder how many times I have said things in private that were in fact recorded and will be used against me when the time comes, because, despite being truthful, it might prove to be inconvenient. I must ask myself though, am I always honest in my statements? Do I never twist the truth? Do you?

FOURTEEN- Health

Health:

"Well-being. Being free from illness or injury, in both the physical and psychological sense. Also, having a state of bodily function near the median values of the age category range standard" (from the 'Over the Counter Remedy Box' Dictionary)

The cornerstones

Health is, by all means, a big definer of our civilization. Do not think otherwise. Do not listen to all the contradicting "hard data" on the subject. We are healthy and we improve this state by the day. All we need to look at is the capabilities and endurance of the new generation, as compared to the latter in every household.

Medicine, as the pillar science to our well-being, has come a long way. It has been a consistent pace, with several fortunate jumps, upon which we continue to base our health. Our life expectancy depends chiefly on it.

At the beginning, the discovery of animalcules which brought germs into the picture. Then, all the counter-controls such as vaccination and inoculation, pasteurization, the use of antitoxins and the, now common, antiseptic and sanitation practices.
Discoveries as penicillin or sulfas made possible the fight against bacteria. Today, antivirals are also joining the drug-based health recovery from illness.
There is a continuous study of illnesses, its causes, spreading mechanisms, its effects and possible cures. Research does not end, it multiplies. Yet to find out, the gigantic step, that sequencing and mapping of the human genome will bring.

Along the road, nutrition has explained, in great detail, our metabolism, our caloric intake and the body building blocks. It has given us a balanced diet of the macronutrients and explained the effects of minerals and vitamins in our body.

All these general discoveries are part of our common knowledge, have a place in our everyday life, from early vaccination to vitamin intake, an ordinary hand washing or hot cooking, all at once.

Outside the medical science, food canning and preservation, beside refrigeration, have, without doubt, enhanced our health. We also have better foods and improved crops. For sure, pure water, controlled waste water and managed solid waste.

Without health, our world would not be as populated. We have tackled a problem and created another one -we´ll see about that later on-. There are nevertheless issues regarding our particular view of health.

Health comes in a flask

The first mistake we have is that health comes as a prescription from a physician. We have forgotten that prevention is what makes the sound condition feasible, that avoiding injury is the complementary route.
We have turned to pharmaceutical products to achieve what we think is health. No, we must remember hand washing, sanitation and a balanced diet. "Consult your doctor," we're advised. "Have regular check-ups," we are instructed. We are thrown to think that health is at the *surgeries* and the pills, not in our habits, wrong.

Some years ago, I met a very old man -eighty eight or nine at the time- who was a regular at the neighborhood supermarket. He always drove himself there. You would have never guessed his age. He didn't look young, just not his age. His mobility was outstanding. His independence and perfect mental state was remarkable. He never turned down help with his groceries to the trunk of his car. From there on, he was on his own. Before getting in the car, he would take just a moment to take out some money, with a slightly shaking hand, he would turn to the boy helping him and, with a very nice smile and a straight look in the eye, would say an earnest 'thank you, till next time'.

One day I spotted him waiting in the drugstore line.
"Hello, is there something wrong?"
"Hello. No, why should it? He answered.
"Well, I mean. You're getting some prescription."
"Oh. It's nothing, just something for my cholesterol," he explained.
I didn't know what to reply. It was odd, but expected at the same time. "Do you have high cholesterol? The good, the bad? You know? Trying not to intrude further.
"On my last check-up," he said.
"And before?" I asked astonished.

It turned out he had outlived three of his regular doctors, and a brand new one thought wise to do a full run, finding several things wrong including his vision and the obviously mistaken – to the doctors belief- habit of drinking nothing except for a glass of cold sparkling water, a bowl of soup at lunch time and a cup of tea in the middle of the afternoon. Too little fluids.
When I heard that, I couldn't but laugh and said the doctor was wrong. That it was him that needed help and prescriptions. I asked him, what would happen to him with high cholesterol in thirty-year's time! What had his low water drinking done to his health in practically ninety years! Why would he have to leave his every morning fried egg, because a new age doctor was prescribing a diet, I assume for a long life –based on the new human swivel stats-.
Two years after, he died from grief, after his younger boy died in a car accident, nothing related to that, unthoughtful, maliciously handled, full check-up.

Years back, to wipe out the mosquito population to fight malaria, DDT was widely used as an innocuous substance to humans, though quite deadly for the anopheles -cool name, although it means *useless*, perhaps it could be shout as an insult-. It was sprayed everywhere. It solved the spread of disease and it is still in production today, but not everywhere, because it turned out not to be harmless. It endangered water life, birds, other insects besides the anopheles, and –you guessed it- also humans. At some point it was declared a neurotoxin and now a carcinogen. But then, it was the non-plus-ultra of pesticides.

Believe me it is not the only case of a remedy that claims will cure your future problems. Often, the pharmaceutical and chemical corporations will place on the market something *you need* that you were far, very far, from knowing you needed.
A new study comes by, showing levels of that protein, or that metabolic chemical in your body, that were never measured before and, yes, you are sick, you need to take a pill for as long as...for the rest of your days. You've been trapped. You've been had.

The new diet

About the same happens with our diet. We are not supposed to eat dozens of things, all of them quite lethal on the long run. Just remember that salt is not good for you, neither are flour or sugar, in fact none of the carbohydrates, please refrain from ingesting it. Same goes for fats. Be careful with proteins. You will die thin, very slender. You can´t have alcohol, no beer, no wine, no liqueur. Certainly drink all the water you want –bottled even better, to avoid all the harmful minerals-, at least four pints a day, to be healthy.

Every now and then, a new theory about nutrition makes its way to our tables, wipes out butter, places in margarine, to later find out that nothing really changed. Takes away cheese and other milk derivatives harming the dairy farmer and your good life, because you are used to eating all of that, so very tasty.

The sugar industry is having a party lately, while the chemical sweeteners take a stand -are we really sure about its innocuity?-. How about the farmers using other types of pesticides –not the infamous DDT-, improved seeds or simple urea or ammonia to fertilize the soil? They are delivering poison, right? We need organic crops, organic processes, ending up with more expensive products, with a shorter shelf life 'no preservatives added'. Great!

Trends, vogue and trends. We are easily lead anywhere, the internet being the battleground for the market. We learn everything there. We apply it right away, because that will kill us, that will develop an illness and that will cripple us. We do not realize that if something is easy to find and expand in the internet is, almost always, not true. Truth is harder to find. It takes an effort.

In the end, we become obsessive of what we eat, or guilty at best. Your diet has been tampered for good. No fun, no life.

The X's Syndrome

I am sure you have heard about the X's syndrome, at least some pages ago. Studies show that every adult is prone to develop this malady in the early fifties, women with a lesser probability. Two thirds of the population will have acute symptoms by the year 2031 –we really have it coming-. There is no treatment available in the market today, but researchers are confident they will come with a cure before the fatal date. Meanwhile, we better take a look at the other ghostly syndromes of our time.

Someone discovers a trait in a group of people, in a region and, through a quick study, concludes a pathological state. They are not bored. They are not working long hours and show fatigue. No, they have a syndrome, requiring medical attention through therapy and some sort of drug. Consumers beware.

Most of the time people lack happiness, lack goals, have no dreams to pursue, leading into various unhealthy states. We are complex beings. It is in our nature to go through rough times with a pain in the chest that seems never ending or a recurrent headache that pounds during the night stealing our sleep. Some so called syndromes could in fact go away with a bowl of chicken soup and a smile.

FIFTEEN- The greedy society

Greed:

"Eagerness to possess something far beyond a need, mainly material items such as money, power and things" (from the 'Greed is not a Sin' Dictionary)

Society:

"Civilization. People living together, interacting peacefully and willingly under common rules and values, traditions and expectations" (from the 'Man is a Social Animal' Dictionary)

Greed

Do we all want to be famous and rich? It may depend on the age group towards whom the question is addressed. But there would be no mistake in answering: yes. Our ideal for starters is to be rich. It is the only way in our world to prove we have accomplished something in life. It is the sign of success. Actually, is there another way to be successful? Oh yes, I almost forgot. To be famous, to be a trending topic, disregarding the reason that brought us under the spot light.

Greed, not happiness, not the joy of being useful –don't laugh at me, please-, not the sight of a family reunion where we are appreciated and loved and reciprocally return the feeling to those seated at the table, not either a life without triumph nor defeat, where nothing happened but a peaceful existence.

We are competitors and we play to win, to be more than the others. We do not contend on deeds such as being friendly – followers on the net, we do- or having the safest street, do not either compete in being a warm-hearted welcoming town. We do not race in being the best neighbor, nor being the most helpful person at work.

Those are not achievements, and no medals are awarded to the best mother or the best father. It is even difficult to define a best parent if the success grading has little to do with money. You are a loving parent and raised a responsible community driven good kid. So what? Where is that kid now? Is she some kind of CEO? Is he an entrepreneur of a billion dollar company? Are they worth several millions at the least? What? You are telling me that all they have is a nice family and are well liked in their home town? Losers, losers, losers. The first "L" is for you as parents, the second one for them as failures and the third one for their children, who have a long way to climb to the top, if they want to leave that disappointing life.

You turned out to be a genius or may have an outstanding knowledge in History, Biology or Astronomy. You, on the other hand, master three languages, including a dead one that has enabled you to translate three scrolls dated one thousand years. Well, you both will be respected, but not necessarily be considered successful until your capabilities turn into bank figures.

We almost have the Midas effect, we turn every valuable thing only into gold, if it cannot be converted, then it is not valuable.

"Hey! My son got into Soldsmund Tech, one of the fifteen best universities, got a summa-cum-laude award. Now he is a top engineer at 'Neurone' the leading computer manufacturer." "How much does he make?" Will be the first question you'll hear. Anything else is not impressive.

"My daughter started a business on her own, up-state. Something to do with fashion and clothing. She has now twenty guys working for her, in only two years!" "What's the revenue?" You will be asked,

"My boy went on a sports scholarship at U-State. He has just been drafted, he has become a pro. Aín't that som'thin?" "How big is his contract?" Will be the unexpected reply.

"How much you wanna bet." That is a usual way to settle a difference in thoughts that remains to be proven. We don't want to take away or dent the honor, the value of the word of others, the importance of their knowledge. No, we want to take away what hurts: money.

I can go on and on trying to prove the value of other values aside from money but our civilization only favors currency and assets -the size of your accomplishment is the size of your wallet-. Our minds are set on greed, it is the main engine of our civilization. It is the bottom line that counts. The figures on the bottom line, that is.

So, if you have in mind to be an educated and prepared person, a good person, to have a nice family, to be well liked in your community, if you desire to help others, to be dependable, you are bound to be placed aside, because you do not belong in this society. Not greedy enough.

The un-society

While you think about the importance of other values –I know you simply don't agree, but I am just and idealist-, while you think about or disregard my comments, leave a little room for this: we are not a society as such, we are an un-society.

Usually a society has common objectives and –yes you're right we have many common objectives and traits: freedom, justice, equality, and so on-...you leave me speechless.
We could be a society, but we do have greed in common, which is way far from a solidarity value needed to assemble a society.
You see, a society does not compete for the right to have a better life, instead it works together for it. A society does not prey on their own, it helps them, protects them. Instead, we

are only a human group, as a gang of predators looking over the fence to find out what can be stolen from the other side. The other side –you may have imagined- are the other human groups. We take advantage of those other groups, to obtain the most we can, just in order to fulfill are need of greed, as a means to prove ourselves within our group.

Since being a brotherhood is not in our rule book, before hunting outside our walls, we bite each other, either as a preparation or because it is basically in our nature –while strolling your street this afternoon, take a peek behind, from time to time, you never know-.

Think about it, money making is at the top of our aims, making it impossible not to do it at the expense of others within our group. We are bound to fail as a true society. We have been lucky enough, for there have been others outside our civilization's fence. As long as they will be beyond our boundary, we will be able to accomplish this dream of enrichment, without the need to prey on our friends, but the world is closing. We have sold our ideas to the world. The antagonist groups are beginning to think likewise. They have become a threat. They are greedy and are trying to get back at us. They are not as feeble as before. I could be wrong, maybe they are not avenging anything, maybe...they learned too well.

I used to be very naïve –don't say it, you believe I still am-. On one occasion a friend approached me to start a business. We were going to be partners and, since I did not have any capital, we agreed I would set up and run the business while he would place the capital –ever heard of that?-. The business he had in mind was a small manufacture. He had figured out the place and even a rough idea of the sales team. He wanted me mostly to handle production.

Once I gave it a thought I told him that we should start by commercializing the products not by manufacturing them. Things went smoothly. I was organizing the warehouse and the team activities when suddenly he proposed me a salary.

"There is no need, we are partners," I explained smiling at him. "Why would I want money that comes from the same pocket?" Then it dawned on me: I was out. He was offering me a job, not a partnership. "Why?" I asked.

"Well…we were going to manufacture, remember?

"Yes, so?"

"You were to take care of that."

"We switched. We made a different business," I explained the evident.

"You have a new role now. Not the same"

It was a long argument. At the end there were two phrases:

"I thought we were friends," I complained.

"Business is business," he concluded.

SIXTEEN- The capital

Capital:

"Money and realizable assets owned by an individual or an organization, a state or country included. Also, wealth" (from the 'How Worthy Are You?' Dictionary)

Capitalism:

"An economic subsystem characterized by trade and industry operating for profit, with monopoly or oligopoly control on prices, production, goods distribution and markets, and money value continuously declining due to sustained and sometimes increased interest rates on savings and credit -also monopoly or oligopoly controlled-.
Mistaken and wrongly said to be a social, economic and political system characterized by private ownership of the means of production and services as opposed to being state owned; trade being determined by free market competition; money value determined by financial markets and investment opportunities" (from the 'Tales From a not so Distant Past' Dictionary the 2087 Ed)

Money doesn't buy happiness

I have three friends that have, and still, devote their lives to aid people. People in distress after catastrophes –such as floods or earthquakes- or people in need –either homeless or in extreme poverty, where everything is needed-. At their tiny organization, throughout the year they collect clothing, medicines, water, toys and money, and throughout the year they deliver this by themselves to the people in need. In critical times, they intensify their work, but seldom participate on government sponsored or managed programs. Countless despairing stories arise from this periodic encounters, involving all ages. Sometimes I wonder the kind of heart one must have to keep on doing this self-appointed penurious task, while most of us rather decide to turn our heads and shut our ears.

Is their struggle very successful, you may ask? No, probably not. They do change the fate of a few and encourage others. They also become the pity and scorn of many others.

A woman in this group told me, one day, about one episode at an earthquake devastated town, a very poor township -so that you might say disaster struck over debris-.
On a particular day, on her way from the public aid camp to the town she noticed a girl -eight or nine year old-, with a ragged dress selling pinwheels at the side of the road. She got off the van and exchanged a few words with the girl, bought a colorful pinwheel and blew softly at it. When she got back on the van she was in tears, but didn´t say a word.
On the next day, she spent a long time shuffling through the collected items to distribute that day, and came upon something she liked.
"A box! I need a box" She cried to the others.
"A box? Who cares about a box?" Someone answered, she told me.
She found the box and placed the object inside, then wrapped it on some printed paper she grabbed from the ground.
While driving the same road as the day before, she was anxious, hoping the girl would still be there. She was.
She stepped out, ran towards the girl and gave her the box, but didn´t do more, time was pressing.
On their way back late that day, the girl was still there proudly wearing a pair of glowing pink plastic sandals that were just a perfect fit. Her smile was that of happiness, worth a million tears.

'Money doesn't buy happiness' is all, but a right statement, because money buys well-being, which is the first step towards happiness. In the beginning, money bought those sandals.

For the homeless, money can buy shelter, clothing and food. Health is beyond their short reach. A warm bath is also excluded.
'Hey, don't worry, money doesn't buy happiness," go and candidly tell him.

'Best things in life are free' is another statement as perverse as the happiness one. Can you recall a soft drop of a light summer rain falling in your face? Yes, you probably can, because you do not live in a cardboard home with dirt floors, where any rain can´t be welcome. Money also buys a house, the kind you have, so that, from your perspective, a light rain is just among the free best things of life, where happiness is not paid.

Looking at the wonder of that mountain from the cozy chalet and the fire place costs money. The feeling is quite different when you have to endure that scenery without proper clothing.

'Money buys everything, happiness included' is a truer statement.

The propaganda about money not being able to buy happiness comes from several perceptions.

One angle, from the wealthy people, is that although they have the money they still are not happy. If they had their money drained, they would agree, in most of the cases, that they were happy before or at least not as unhappy. It is convenient for this class, however, to tell everyone the lack of impact of money, so that the threat to their capital is lessened.

Another viewpoint comes from the poor that, despising the rich, momentarily disregard money, to relish on the few obstacles and headaches encountered by the rich, proving that money isn't everything.

On those suffering from anxiety, stress, anger or simply the lack of love is very easy to remind themselves that money is not solving any of their problems. It is so ineffective, that the conclusion is that money is worthless in things that count.

Don't fool yourself, money is the basis of happiness. Money represents your personal trading power –or a nation's-. All your effort is converted into a currency that allows you to exchange your work for goods, to fulfill your family and personal needs. Happiness starts there, where your wage is sufficient to deliver a good life. Your accomplished job turns into joy. Well, sometimes it doesn't because your wage is low and your shift-output is considered worthless within the system.

"All of your activities in this company are important," any CEO will say.
"Your jobs are needed, highly appreciated and a complement to the bigger task we all have set for ourselves. We are proud to be one of the biggest players in our field. Congratulations. Thank you."

"Nice speech. How about a complementary appreciation on my paycheck?" Crosses your mind.

There are shades of wealth within our western way of life, rich and not so rich countries. In one case, at ease with your life, money is not a problem, but in another...
Can you feel happiness without money? Only briefly for 'money doesn't buy happiness'.

The true face of the capital: added value

When seen from a distance, it appears that capitalism is defined by private ownership. I believe this to be wrong. Capitalism is defined by its purpose, rather than by its ownership. Take for instance some of the big state-owned energy companies, that lay out their business plans to play in the capital world by all the rules and guidelines as any other energy company privately owned. How is that different? Their goal is not to provide energy till the last lost corner of the nation is covered for, it is instead to be a profitable enterprise.

How about banking? In my opinion banks are the best ambassador to capitalism. To no one's surprise, countries have state-owned banking that lays out their business plans to play in...-sorry I am repeating myself-. So much for the private ownership.

On the other hand, where is the dividing line between private and public? One, two, fifty, a thousand shareholders? How private!

No, not the proprietorship, capitalism is rather *that*, that appertains to capital –I am really sharp today-. One must ask, what is it essential to capital? What is it that belongs only to capital?

Capital is no longer that trade token, that old and extinct exchange mechanism. No, it is '*the capital*', a spider of a different kind in the animal kingdom.

Appreciation, added value, capital gain, *plus-value*, that is the first of the only two definers of capitalism. The capital grows on its own. It's alive. One coin becomes a unit and a fraction, then the unit plus the fraction become more fractions. Coins multiply following the compound interest rate. They grow geometrically. If we could use this compound trick by the millisecond, we would accelerate its progress even more –microsecond you proposed?-.

Capital growth is inherent to capital –obvious right?-. It is what moves capitalism. It reproduces depending on the circumstances, more or less favorable to establish, to dictate, the interest rate size, it is not globally fixed. It is regulated by the power of the money itself and the country in question. If a government is weak enough, banking and the business operation will place that rate in two digits, no sweat. In some other places it may be kept at bay, just one digit. In extreme case out of control, it will explode. By the power of the sacred free market it will settle for as much as possible. All the capital players will go along with it.

Capital prevails

Towards where does the money flow in the world? To the highest interest rate paying country available –I meant to say to the most favorable emerging market-. It has an instinct to go there. It senses where to land.
Capital has an RNA code. It is drawn to the core of the organism and uses its resources until depletion. As a result, it replicates and uses even more and more genetic material from the host –you're right, money-, afterwards moves unto the next host. Brilliant, it's a virus.
Like any other virus it is very hard to kill or expel. It usually departs after the damage has been done and the host is no longer suitable for reproduction. Also, as the viruses, it can remain for periods of time awaiting, dormant you would say, unchanged, never undermined, its latent power ready to act.

Capital takes control of those banking or bourse organisms. It also works its way through corporations, but the real astounding feature is that feasts on people. Once you are touched by it you become its slave. It changes your mind. It PO$$E$$E$ you, it prevails –If you have opened this book on a reader with the availability to correct the spelling, you will be as amazed as I was that PO$$E$$E$ is not marked as a misspelled word, neither is Capital$-.

Capital is so strong that whole governments trust in it its possibilities of progress and society development. That´s where the expectations are placed, not on work, not on production, not on goods, just in cash. The sound of shuffling bills or ringing coins is truly powerful.

Capital, the leasable asset

Capital can be regarded as an asset. Under that name, it can be leased and rented as any other asset, I suppose. There are car rentals, boat rentals, house rentals, land, planes, tuxedos, warehouses, excavators…well, anything of your choice. If there is an asset, there is a leasing possibility.

Someone could say that rent in itself is a payment for doing nothing, as if pointing out a low moral value in it or just a lacking one.
In fact, people can use their acquired wealth, converted into a good, to be lent to somebody else for a price. That price generally involves covering the depreciation of the goods, the evident time that the owner cannot use it, plus some extra amount. The same thing goes on with money, except for one big change: money doesn't wear out.
Don't you just love having something that never deteriorates? That lasts forever? When money is leased the rent is just for growth, since it will be replaced entirely, perhaps laundered if it was filthy.

Let's assume, for the moment being, that we understand and accept that logic for the basic rent. How in the world is compound interest thrown in? Beats me. Compound interest to infinity, really?
If we are to play with math, why don't we square it, along with a risk explanation or whatever we may imagine, to make it stick? Certainly compounding is a very different story.

Back to the leasing. If we have the money, but not much to do with it, we have to rent it. Right? There will always be someone in need. As an example, in the real estate business, a house can be leased even with cockroaches if the need is powerful enough -"I'll have the roof repaired if you move in." Word of honor from your brand new landlord, showing you around-.

The easiest way to rent your money is by placing it in the bank. The riskiest way is the stock exchange market –beautiful name, I shiver every time I pronounce it-. You can also become the street corner money lender. In the bank you will have a fixed rate, but if you invest your earnings –sorry, your gains- you will get a compound gain. Make your choice.

There is some other way to play math that, at times, rivals the compounded rate, please welcome the variable rates.

"There you go. Just sign in here and here, and we are all set," is your financial executive, leading you through the contract – tiny footnotes and all-. Nice office, decent coffee.
"I still worry about the variable clause," says your wife and co-signer.
"Don't worry," interjects your appointed executive. "Things have been stable. Remember it can also go down, not just up," he explains her, as she turns to find the gaze, above the not so perfect suit. A grin is there.
"Yes," he offers, "it can go down," then, to reassure both, "if you want, when we're finished here, we can step a moment in my boss's office, Ms. Durot –you've met her-, I am sure she will fully clarify that matter."
Finally, after a calculated pause. The punch comes in. "Right now, is the best mortgage you can get. We never know how long we are going to have this offer. It is very good." You mindlessly keep on signing where the crosses are.
"Ok, all set. Come this way…"

Is like the last minute booking in that resort at the beach of your dreams. 'Buy now, only two places available at this rate.' The amazing thing is that you are pressed just enough to sign now, instead of thinking, 'if things are so stable, why should I rush? Why should this too-good-to-be true rate vanish?'
They are the professionals, their advice is what should be followed. You have the means now, the house tomorrow and, in ten years, the variable rate -dependent on the oil prices, the uranium market, the pineapple flue or a war in some of those corners of the world unknown to you- could unfortunately declare you, foreclosure material, only because you could not foresee or budget the variable value.

Back to the usual rates –drifting too much-. I almost forgot that money does deteriorate. It rusts through inflation, although inflation comes from the interest rate. As big as the interest rate the money decays. It weakens itself. What a predicament! The most unlooked-at paradoxes of our times. No interest rates, no money growth, but no money loss. What's the point then? Well, there is always a chance that I will move my pieces better than others on the board. I may win, they will lose.

Capital growth as the standard

It is over this reproduction capability that most of the personal and business decisions are made.

Just for instance, think about a decision between a house rental or purchase, you actually look at the interest of money as the milestone.

If your annual rent compared to the value of the house falls below the interest rate, most real estate agents will tell you to rent. Otherwise they will advise to not dump your money and invest in the house.

Same holds true for an enterprise feasibility study. Is the outcome of your money, invested in the business, better than the interest rate plus risk? No? Invest it in the bank or the many available options. Your friendly banker can help. Whether it becomes a loan for your project or a bond for your money, they are there to help...for a fee.

Usury

Ouch! A forbidden word slipped through the keyboard. What a strong word. It is as bad as finger-pointing.

Usury is defined by exorbitant rates or by an excess over legal interest rates, by obscene short-term paybacks. It is at the same time defined as an activity *sans scrupules*.

Interestingly, in this western world, as I mentioned before, there are markets where interest rates may have no limit. Those 'no-limits' are above the legal limit of other countries within the un-society, making it the legal practice of usury. Now the question is: if this is a moral issue how much is too much? Or –by analogy-, how large does a robbery has to be to qualify as a robbery? Petty not enough and white collar too much, the crime is just in the middle? I am puzzled again. There are countries where an ATM withdrawal has a cost of instant 6% to 3%. Legal? Certainly. It is the free market. Mortgage rates of 30% to 40%, why not?

Whether good or not, whether needed or exceeded, capital never ceases to grow. That is the first feature of capitalism.

The most wanted side of capitalism: profits/ROI

ROI, the goal of money when not growing by interest rates. First of all, please note that I will not be referring to the stock market, although somehow, it could claim to be related through corporate stock. I will be referring to entrepreneurship, not to the investing of money *per se*. Since the stocks are, in principle, the same as banking interests, there is no use for specific paragraphs. That roller coaster is out of the way and soon –hopefully- to be derailed.

Having that said, let's turn to the other face of capital, which is essentially the same face on a less greedy mode, because capital faces are shaped as those on a ball or a Moebius band. Anyway, this other side is profit, ROI gets involved. Perhaps it is the same thing as interest rate gains, but it is now through a productive usage, not the speculation recently explained. In this case money can be eroded. In the worst case scenario –again using common phrases from the 37th story in the corporate headquarters-, there is a chance of ending at a negative figure with some zeros and commas, so, you better have your bags ready, as well as some shoe box money, for that rainy day. No suits needed on your tropical island exile.

Money used to produce goods and services (G&S) also produces wealth. When you look around in your house or on the street, you may not consider at first your surroundings as wealth, but they are.

Visualize for a moment that you are going down the road to another town, maybe just for the ride. Beautiful colored trees on that fall afternoon and sweet foliage scent, with a tint of soil moisture. Cars passing by, a tractor working on the field. A farm house next to and old barn with a reddish roof...Suddenly there is no car, no road and no trees, there is no wealth.
Our wealth surrounds us, materialized as light bulbs, bikes, phones, board games, books, laptops, furniture, music, food and everything we have for our well-being. Things produced by entrepreneurship. Your landscaping is often part of it.

There is clearly a big difference from the money placed for profit in a productive business than that of the money market. Don't trip yourselves, stock money doesn't necessarily become industries nor its amassed profit.

When we create something we accumulate wealth. Money in that sense, can only do it when converted to G&S, converted to the car on the road, bound to a cup of coffee and a face-to-face chat destination. If it is not used, it becomes as useless as our attic forgotten basketball, because we can no longer jump on the court.

Entrepreneurs, we were discussing. In your business, month after month, after everything has been paid for, you alone or you the shareholder, still have a revenue to collect: the profit. This income is trapped between the cost and the price. You take a look at your costs to find what can be taken out. You also study your prices –perhaps a 3.5% increase will go unnoticed-.

Thus, the capital seeks a low cost operation/location preferably aligned with a high price market/sale, nothing new. If your product requires manpower, you move to a country with low wages. If it requires tons of energy –energy is not measured in tons, but...- you go where electricity, gas or oil are cheap, and so on. Today your market may be far just as long as it is not time consuming –that has been discussed-. Your market could be home, you just manufacture away. Your objective is the objective of the capital, to generate as much profit as possible. If that helps or not your hometown is out of the question. You are in business, not a social service provider.

This greedy behavior already mentioned, defines capital. In no way, from jobs lost to people's death, the capital cares for bystanders or parties involved. Collateral damage is common, but regarded as the natural result of modernity, the 'unwanted' instances along the way of progress. We are confronted once more with a moral situation, not an economic one, but, quite expected, our ethics can shake any economic system.

ROI attained value has varied in time and seems to be evasive. It depends on politics, markets, manufacturing technology, the discovery of new materials, the efficiency improvement…most of all is a personal and collective decision, a human, not a technical decision.
What should the profit be for an entrepreneur? Regardless of the calculations we can have on the cost structure and the margin to market prices, we have to ask ourselves if the prices are right in the first place.

Then, a fact first, prices do not come from the market –what?-. A new product price comes from the cost plus the profit, even if it is competing as a substitute to an existing product. A standard is set at that point. It was fixed hoping for large amounts sold at that profit. When competitors arrive, they already have a price to meet or defeat. Does anybody on that race wish to sell lower, to make less money? Not really, unless they are sure to wipe out the competition. Unwritten accords take place, so that the price benefits all of them. The same thing goes for salaries and the raw materials needed – downsized, certainly-, an untold agreement works for all, to control and maximize profits -Oh! That is what you refer to as 'markets'. I am a fool-.

As in its other side, capital fancies replication, looks forward to the offspring. Projects are not set for returns in 10 or 20 years, they are set for 2 to 5 years, to deplete materials, use people and make profit. The nature of capitalism, again, has nothing to do with free markets nor ownership. It does face competition, but is not a regulatory border, it's a fence to jump in order to conquer, assimilate or destroy the opponent and become a monopoly, although you can always settle for the oligopoly, a draw it is.

As to what do we need profits for, an endless list seems to be at hand. Time given, we can become money hoarders, just to own it, to have it, to prove ourselves, to show off. At some point, is not anything we need, it's our envelope.

But that wrapping is soon to shrink and become a problem for us, not for the already collaterally damaged.

Capital and math: the inconsistency flaw

Can you conceive a stack of banknotes that cannot buy anything? Surely not. That's precisely the flaw of capitalism. It can happen. It has already happened somehow, but it has been swept under the 'crisis' carpet. The fortunate, simple part of its explanation, is that it is just a practical and mathematical inconsistency, not a social or moral forever controversial flaw. Nonetheless, it has been debated over time and will be on the table for quite another two or three generations of humans. What is this dent in the perfect system?

At the limit of the world, where our species will have covered the curved ball and the capital system engulfed the last square mile, at the time when we will not be allowed by our own preservation nature to increase the population, the markets will easily show the following: the fulfillment of the very old quantity theory of money.

I assume I do not have to explain why population growth cannot be infinite, but just to state the point, can you tell me how in the world will an infinite number of people will stand on a square meter, in a finite surface? At some moment the world will stop its population growth and hopefully it will decrease it. I'd be happy enough if today we accepted to live at a zero growth index. Wouldn't you? You don't understand what I'm talking about? No. No! It has nothing to do with not having children! Oh my, oh my! We'll discuss that later.

Think for the moment, that we have a finite production of G&S. Think that we are at that point where no more people demand more than the produced quantities, when no more than the delivered services are needed. We've arrived at a time when the people consume –as they almost always do– just what they need and what they can afford to buy.
It is clear that the amount of services and goods have a value that can only be purchased with money. For that to take place, it is imminent for people to have the money to pay for the G&S. The sum of the purchasable and useable items has to be the sum of the salaries. If this does not occur, for instance that the sum of salaries falls short from the value of the items, then there will be items without a buyer that should have not been produced or generated. On the opposite end, if salaries are beyond the sum of the items, then money will be spared. This is precisely the case of the profits.

Let's put this into simple equations

Quantity of Goods + Available Services = Needs of People

If this is not true, then either we will have lack of produce or excess of it. Not one corporation or individual will produce more than they can sell, neither will they lose the chance to produce what can be delivered. A balance will be met.

This brings us to the next equation

Sellable goods + sellable services = salaries of people

If this is not true then either we will have lack of money or excess of it. Not one corporation or individual will give away product not paid for, neither will people pay extra for the received G&S. If in your mind you're trying to balance the equation, in one case you will produce a devaluation and the items will be more expensive, and in the other an appreciation and the items will be cheaper. A balance will be met.

Where are the profits in all of this? That is extra money that doesn't buy anything. Profits need to be zero for the equation to be balanced.

It is not that I want to force the equations to be real. Think toothpaste or bread. Will you produce and try to sell more toothpaste or bread than needed? No, you wouldn't. More cars, phones, armchairs and clothes? No, there is a limit. But to sell the needed quantities you need a market, a market of users and the users need to have the money to pay. Profits are unusable.

Wealth is present in what you see, in what you use. Money is not wealth, it will reach its uselessness at that limit point of zero growth. Those that will keep the money will not have wealth, they will have a pile of banknotes that can't buy anything.

You are probably thinking that the so called limit will never come or, that at least, is very far. Maybe, you are so attached to profit, that you are trying to find out where the equation is wrong. You need to find out.

The equations are so right, that unfortunately represent the reason for so many unexplained economic behaviors.
You cannot found a theory on economics based on an equation where money generates profit, other than the value of the work involved, or where money grows on its own by the rocket fuel of interest rates.

If you add profit to the equation, the equation is no longer true. The economics of the capital have an inconsistency flaw where:

Profit = Value of Goods and Services – Money paid in Salaries

But -since at the end of population growth the primal equation will come to light-

Value of goods and services = Money paid in salaries

Necessarily means that

Profit = 0

But it is profit we get as large as possible, creating as a result the needed inflation to compensate the equation, along with the social problems that the capital claims to be solving.

Big inflations, big crises, shortages, recessions…all is explained by the equation trying to balance excess profits, trying to check them out. I understand you don't agree. This is not new, though.

Not so long ago, within our West-Civ., in one of those iconic closed markets or almost closed markets, the rich countries exported G&S, while the poor ones imported them. Travelling the same road, the most powerful one invested in the weak ones. It made housing projects on the poor one's lands, for sale and profit. Since there was no money to cover for it all, a loan was placed, but was not paid back. The compound interest accrued the debt and finally some part of it had to be forgiven. The interest rate money had no actual value. Every country within the Union is losing value on their money, awaiting the payments to come, but payments may only be if wealth is produced at those debtor nations. Will it?

There are questioned free-trade agreements world-wide. The countries and the people, the consumers, are not being favored. It is about corporate trade boosting profits and exhausting the savings, ending on huge cuts on the purchasing power of people. It is known as a financial crisis. Why not simply capital crisis?

More than often we are witnesses to the boom of the stock markets. Corporations are overvalued, stock is bought expecting a great profit at the resale.
Shouldn't we see that a company cannot be worth more than its production and assets? The future market you may correct me, but then again, the future market comes down to production and maybe it will require larger production facilities, larger assets. As I said: its production and its assets. The overvalued stock is money growing on thin air that is worth zero.

Face it, it is happening, profits are losing its value. The equation tries to come to balance once in a while, causing those 'crashes'. We must remember that in the end money is an exchange item, not *the* item.

Why is it not crystal clear right now? Besides the cover-up, there are reasons –sorry, what cover-up?-.

There is guilt, a need to conceal the greed, the stealing that profits and interest rates mean. There is a need to explain that you do not prosper because you need to work harder, not that someone has been short-paying you. A necessity to prove that everything is morally right. It's the markets' behavior, something beyond our powers. It's nature, not men. That's the cover-up.

But, as I was saying, there are reasons that hinder the appearance of the flaw.

The first reason is that, since the system is not yet quite closed, not at the end limit, the profits can buy what it is not produced: *id est.* minerals, land...natural resources. It will cushion the effect for a while. However, unlimited resources are a *mirage*. Materials are already being recycled today, at all times because they are economically convenient, but in many cases because the resources are already scarce. It becomes the new type of mining and extractive industries.

The second one is that humanity is still growing, the markets are demanding, but we are not endless, we will be limited. At the moment, this population growth buffers the balance, covers the flaw.

The most evident proof of the balancing of the equation is the unstoppable inflation worldwide. I leave it to you, I do not need to convince myself. I can spare myself the nice speeches from our leaders. I can see the economy through a simpler equation.

The economy and the world, once closed, will drain the last purchasable resources and fade away into balance. And do not dream on mining mars or the moon, if there is money at hand, there will be, alas, no return on investment.

There is something that I must not forget to mention. Not all sales of products and services are purchased by consumers, it seems that I have left out this large portion of exchange between the corporations. No, I have not. In the end, all economic activities come to be a part of the consumers purchase: a commodity converted into an object; energy converted in a household electric flow; water at the faucet or food on the table. All funnels to the consumers. It was discussed before in the GDP. Have you read it? It's boring enough, except for the part where...

The utopic stable capital society

Money had come into the picture as a need, it is yet a need for exchange, but when the capital turns volatile on its own, trade is altered, even more if it involves more than one type of currency, worsened if the currencies lack a stable interchangeable rate.
Money should withstand time passage. It should also have a correspondent fixed trade between countries. For that to be

true, its value and quantity should match the wealth that it represents. Not an easy task, but not so tough since the strong economies are already dealing with it, ruling over the weak ones to fix exchange rates to the milli-unit.

Money, as a token with a standard worth, will still have to face the adjustment in value of the G&S, but there would be no need for our savings account to be placed here or there to compensate for inflation, the personal effort made to earn it would be untouched. Society would be pleased.

How would I generate savings? By working more, by providing more output in products and services, by burning the midnight oil. Got it?

Is it easy to come down to a stable value on the money? No, given the present situation. The future limit-conditions will make it easier. We don't have to do anything. We are among the last generations to deal with the problem.

G&S might not conserve its value, I said. G&S prices may shift due to unfortunate storms destroying plantations, flooding factories and blocking roads and railroads. Foodstuffs may increase as the result of a plague, a virus or other biological or chemical contamination. The trend of supply and demand would still play in the market of stable capital. G&S prices could and should decrease in the face of new more productive technologies.

But for sure, G&S prices will always be in the hands of speculation. It is almost impossible to dehumanize our society.

Because of all this, it is hard to expect a stable capital society, but in time we can narrow the differences. That is a good enough goal or a bright start.

Another obstacle to stability is the wealth gap in the world, which is already there, but enhanced when we conquer - economically speaking- other countries. Since we seek the high profits, we underpay their resources and manpower. At the same time, we sell our capital-and-markets religion, mostly because we want to develop our new niche, not that we want them to change. After the colonization period and having established production lines in their lives, we also teach them our way of life. Once converted, they become a bad copy of ourselves. They begin to strive for the same targets. Our invasion strikes back using our own concepts.

It is preferable to have a stable society? Yes, in fact, despite all my sour ideas, ours is quite stable and average earnings have played a very important role in it. In the first world a manager's wage can be from five to ten times the lowest wage paid inside a corporation. In the western third world it can be a thousand times, how stable is that society? Strikes, unions, agreements, blood, death, *scabs*, have modeled the shape that our corporations have nowadays. Is it perfect? No, but it is metastable. Capital stability will, with certitude, provide a better living standard and we will be an improved society.

The displaced capital interest, the displaced profit

Today in our front yard, profit and interest rates are being displaced, set aside. For many, a good wage is enough. In other cases it is the only way to go, you don't think so?

A farmer with today´s technology for seeds, fertilizers, weather forecast, machinery and storage, is able to tend several hundred acres of land for cereal crops. He may call it profit, but at the end of the year, when he collects the revenue from the only sale of the period, what he has in hand is his yearly wage, nothing more.
His oldest daughter may have a feeling to pursue the same occupation, just as he did from his parents. Regretfully, she will need more land to get her yearly wage, since they cannot both survive on the same output. They end up acquiring more hectares or unfortunately renting those acres.
They've been working generation after generation in a world where profits are not met, only wages. On the contrary, they suffer from the interest rate of the money lenders to make

ends meet during the year, suffer as well the blow from the surface rental that short-slices their wage. Finally another skimming process shrinks their wage: the unknown selling price for their crop. Which way to go? Futures? Spot? Insurance? In any case, for all the troubles to tackle, if the surface worked is ample enough, they live comfortably well on wages.

Other farming produce may require more or less people. A vineyard, depending on its size, may employ a dozen or a couple hundred. The function sets the needs.
A dairy farm or poultry farming, may also face different number of employees.

A trend has begun to avoid the hurdles discussed with the cereal farmer: Coops. Laborers own the farm, each with a function and a wage. The farm may belong to a conglomerate of farms that own a small regional bank. It also has a distribution network and regional markets as the end point to the consumer. The trade is done within the region. The wealth is distributed within the region. The common interest rates and profits are not really present, but good wages are. Function sets the needs, the people and the wages. You will be surprised when you search and find the number of people on Coop farming and the huge volumes that are produced.

In our modern world, sometimes it started with a strike that went into bankruptcy, leading to the closing of the factory. The union had a wise idea: 'now that everything is lost to us and the owners, let's propose a purchase'. The union bought the place and resumed operations. Same middle management, same employees, same wages and no loss. The bankruptcy had to do more with the lack of profits than the actual lack of feasibility, but these people do not need the profits, they need the wages.
Some other times it has started with a blunt proposal from the employees, at the moments when the markets are receding. These are peaceful takeovers from those who need the income. Again, look it up, be surprised by the number of people employed this way today.

There is another case: all of those trades that the big industry and the supermarket chains started to wash away, but that, resilient to the times and pushing through quality craftsmanship are still standing. Blacksmiths, silversmiths, carpenters, electricians, bakers, tailors, plumbers, upholsters, masons, mechanics, gardeners and many other trades co-exist in our society with the big firms, working independently and receiving not profit, but their wage.

I bet that the absence of interest rates and profit, meant for you, reader, some catastrophe. Don't fear the end of capitalism, since it is not the end of private property nor the end of your way of life. It is just the end of the leeches. It is neither the end of freedom. All the above people and cases have quite freely decided their fate and live better than before and could even improve that.

The economic system, regardless of the social system –yes, regardless of the social system-, is very simple. It boils down to a cost structure as related to the production process and its functions. You will always have a facility of some sort, based on a process that will need and use raw materials –for a bakery, mining, farming or tire manufacturing-, energy and wages. There is a price in the market and a calculation of a break-even point. If you don't have the production to get there, to break even, then your trade or company or occupation is not feasible despite the social system.

The capital, in contrast, is a moral standing, not a social system, although it shapes or deforms one to feed from it. It confounds us portrayed as an economic system, rather being a sub-system. The best biological analogy of the capital in our economic system is that of a parasite in your intestines.

I know, I know, you've been told marvels of capitalism and thought that democracy, freedom, health were caused by it. Well, it is your 21st century wake up call. Capitalism has, instead a very black history.

Capitalism as that moral posture, at some time promoted slavery, it founded company-stores, it established 12 hour a day shifts, low wages, child labor and it has ended in organized crime, just for the sake of profit.

What social changes are required to depart from profit and interest rates? None. Just to proscribe it will do. Your private and social life need not modify. Your personal effort will be distinctively rewarded. Your earnings will be preserved. Now, if by any chance you wish to associate, you will be confronted with your fellowmen and the so-human-weakness of lack of solidarity, but then maybe you will be lucky or skillful enough to find true business partners, feel *free* to do it.

Must we change the structure and operation of our government? Only if you want, but not for the purpose of controlling interest rates or profit. Should our bureaucracy be erased? No, it should be in all cases shrunk or enlarged to meet the function requirements as any other job. Bureaucracy is useful, you know?

How about the free market and competition? What about G&S prices? Well I answer, what about them? Leave it the way it is. That is not the major problem here. Markets disrupt the balance very little. Once you lift greed from the equation even speculation is less likely to appear. Example exerts a greater pull than law enforcement, I believe. You need not rule on all, people will settle to a better coexistence, will bite less at each other.

More than once, to my fortune, I have visited our big cities. Some of its main parks, fountains and alleys are just a perfect relaxing view. The skyline is breathtaking. There is a sense of greatness. Alternatively, in the same cities, there are filthy subway stations –inside and out-, where, as a visitor, you feel uncomfortable and, as a local, as I take it, you get used to it. In both cases there is a constant, the pull of example. In one place you feel compelled to use the wastebasket and in another you don't mind to litter.

The people living on wages, just like you, never had use for profits and could do without the interest rates. A CD means for you a compact disk, not a certificate of deposit —have you ever heard that one?-. You are a part of another subsystem not the capital one. Imagine your chance to nip at a very small percentage of the existing profits converted into wages, before the rest is lost in the wind, where it belonged. Imagine the example of those in the free world working proudly for wages, exploiting no one.

We readily adapt to safety and comfort, to beauty and wealth. How could you not adapt to a higher income as a result of a lower cost to your life doing exactly the same thing you are already doing? Think about it.

The signs of the times

Are the regional markets and Coops the early dismantling process towards economic balance? Is the economic world crisis nothing but the adjustment to balance? Are the disrupted societies of the second, third world —fourth and fifth, for that matter-, the result of the activities and interference of the first world? I leave that for you to debate. My answer is yes to all counts.

Over time, voices have come and revolutions have supported those claims, but again and again the system has replaced itself. It has rebuilt. I only believe that it is approaching its limit, that there is an unavoidable trend. The system has trenched itself, protected with barbed wire, it will have more walls, drones and land robots to guard its premises, but it will eventually have to, in order to subsist in at least a minute form, *repartir antes que morir*.

EPILOGUE TO THE FOUNDATIONS

The foundations are connected, they are not isolated traits. They manifest as a whole, intertwined like in a nonwoven cloth, making a solid complex hard to tear. They cannot be seen one without the other. We believe them indivisible.

We are told and taught axioms of life. We conveniently believe in them, it is, after all, our cradle, nourishment and joy. Sometimes we are frustrated and feel for a moment that we've been deceived. Glimpses of a different truth, of a conflictive axiom, of a new archetype. We rebel in action or thought. Perhaps we don't have the bigger picture, maybe we are not meant to have it.

In the end we are in need of guidance and must live as a healthy group, a stable society... we need to look up at somebody but should refrain from infatuation... it is illogic to grant us a democracy but It is indispensable to have justice... it is convenient to have freedom and be heard...It is immoral, inconsistent, economically disruptive to praise the capital, by having interest rates and high profits...we do require to be productive...all of this in order to achieve personal and common wealth and happiness.

It is hard to grasp that the system is not as good as it looks.

PART II
SHOCKWAVES

PART II
SHOCKWAVES

ONE- Arrogance

Arrogant:

"Feeling superiority over others and showing it by exaggerating our importance, our capabilities and influence, looking down upon others and lacking respect for them" (from the 'Self-made Human' Dictionary)

How would the foundations shatter? With natural shockwaves, that is. The first one of them is our arrogant behavior. We can't help it we...are...the...best! We are the benchmark, the lead, the paradigm, the guide, the light, the summit of mankind. Need I say more?

Several empires –civilizations if you wish- that preceded us, stood in the same position as we do today. What makes us different? Well we are...we! The snappy answer inside our heads and at the tip of the tongues. Other civilizations have succumbed to this popularity contest and because of it. We will not, someone thinks, since the rest of us do not even consider a chance of failure. How can perfection fail?

Our mistakes start by acknowledging that we have the state of the art science and the scientists that create it, the belief that we, the common people, are part of those accomplishments. However, the fact that we benefit from the applied use of the newest discovery does not make us a part of it, just its lucky depositaries. We profit on every science advance. Science, turned into process technologies and goods, gives us a better life that, in the light of our positive or negative involvement in our society, we may or not deserve, but we are not that science and those are not our ideas, our realizations. We are much smaller. Taking the credit for the creations of a tiny group, of wise and dedicated people, doesn't make us bright. Dumb we stand before them.

As a human group, we don't listen, thus, we don't learn. A couple hundred nations in the globe have a lot say, a lot to teach, just not to our shut hearing. By specializing in our frame of thought, we become ignorant. We believe we are the handlers of truth, our way of life being the only one to cherish and pursue, our values the sole means for happiness, development and human cohabitation. The way we house families, how we teach our young, how we stratify our society, our goods and wrongs are the way to be. Our morals are the only beacon in the dark shadows of human progress, so we think.

We do not probe, neither learn other cultures or their languages. They should adjust to our own, despite millenary differences, regardless of geographical or social conditions, despite proven wisdom risen from those other humans. Our religions, that we do not truly observe -fire would rain on us for our continuous blasphemy, not that I care, but since we say we honor the holy word...-, our creeds, I was saying, are the code to follow, we make mocking remarks, now and then, over other's beliefs and behaviors, we ridicule their routines, their practices. We simply lack the smallest respect for cultures unlike our own. We find them lesser, minor, destroyable, replaceable, which we readily do or set ourselves to doing, after all, the truth shall set them free, *our truth!* Right?

We judge all other communities from our vantage point provided by the most powerful militia and subdue them, never allowing them to take a stand.

We waste resources, living the life of plenty. We trash things as soon as they have fulfilled the primary objective for which we produced them. We have erased forests, wiped out rivers and land, to now flag the defense of nature, habitats and ecosystems.

On our every day, ordinary life, we "renew", do not preserve what we have. When was the last time –or would it be better to ask for the first?-, that you cleaned a sparkplug, calibrated it and screwed it back in place? The last time you changed the sole of your shoes instead of buying new ones? The last time you fixed your toaster or coffee maker instead of getting a spare? The last time you decided that your old phone or computer do not need a replacement, but a repair? The last time you patched something?

My peace of mind shows up on the horizon, because we cannot be repaired either. The ones that will follow, the upgraded humans, the generation to come, will replace us right after using us and discarding us. What a relief. They have the same DNA you say? We're condemned, then.

We do not read, despite the remarkable writing and printing output –another paradox of our times-. We want it easy: video and sound. We do not want to reflect on things, we need it summarized. We don´t want several views, we love quick and easy answers to question we do not pose. We are very opinionated. Our attitude is presumptuous and decisive. The smallest enlightenment we deny.

We have been doing the very same things that previous empires, former brilliant civilizations, have done. We are paving the same road in the same manner, because 'all roads lead to…us'. We are building over the debris of the cultures we stomp but do not quite vanish. We bully them, expecting no answer but allegiance. What was the fate of all other civilizations? Which *caligae* ours is wearing? Why are those people not here today? How could time wash them off? Arrogance was the first step.

We do not conceive that something could go wrong, mainly due to the fact that, 'effortlessly', we maintain our rule over the world. We are wrong, with great and sustained determination we are where we are, with an unfortunate angle, our influence is declining, our grip is weakened, but, arrogant we, we don't notice it.

The coach rolled slowly along the slim road, dividing the sandy landscape. Once in a while, it would almost stop, to smoothly pass over sand bumps, left by the wind the day before. It followed a caravan of buses -all air conditioned and fitted with large stained windows, protecting the tourists from the heat and brightness of the noon hour-.

"Look at those kids playing in the dirt. Shouldn't be at school?" And before any answer could be given, "that's why they don't prosper." Kept the young woman pointing out, "Is this what we fight for? Is this why we give our sons to the world?"
"But."
"Look, look!"
"It's the holiday's ma'am," said an old man sitting alongside. "Besides, that is a very clever game they're playing."
"What? That!" She replied.
"Yes, it is played with-"
"So? We're here to see the pyramids," she interrupted, "I can't see this is what's left of the great people that built the pyramids," and eying her neighbor, "a plague maybe? I heard it was a cataclysm. What happened?"
"Don't know," he answered, while the bus kept going on the long ride to the ruins.

No, you didn't get to know what the game was about, nonetheless I agree, it is quite clever.

Yes, we set them free from their rulers, from their twisted traditions, from their upside-down economies and bogus goals. We fight to liberate them, we set the new targets: growth, free markets, education, manufacturing jobs...consumption and consumption –I wrote it twice? It's all right, three times would have been too many-. Arrogant us, we truly think we are needed. We're not. We could stay behind the barbed wire compound we call home.

TWO- The greater good

Greater good:

"Worthy and useful for the majority. Beneficial and approved for the society as a whole. Reasonable and competent decisions for the common wellbeing" (from the 'Let's Leave the Rest Behind' Dictionary)

We have to sacrifice for the common interest, for social welfare, for the greater good. Do we? We see, now and then, our individual rights overturned or violated in favor of that greater good.

We have been taught to fear social movements, people's empowerment trends, to dislike parity by force, yet we are immersed more and more in doing for the sake of others at our own expense. Freedom is lost, liberty is compromised and justice is not really served. Quite a shockwave.

I was standing at a street corner, waiting for the stop light to grant me permission to cross, along with many other pedestrians and cars heading the same way, while other pedestrians and vehicles passed in front of us. 'A computer system controls our doing and we don't even wink,' I thought. In that case, however, my individual rights were not restrained –I think-, because that willingly accepted red light and the rule behind it, protected me from harm. I was rather advised not to walk, nor impeded, since I could have taken a step forward, rightfully ending my life under a truck's wheels. By doing so, I would have endangered the liberty rights of the truck driver.
A system designed to delay my rights, extend my life and keep me from fighting my way through city traffic and pedestrians. Not a bad deal. All of us comply, all of us benefit immediately from it.

Some other occasion, during harvest time, I was cruising a rural road recently opened, when I had to step on the brakes, due to a wide patch of mud and straw left by a tractor that had been crossing in the morning. Before we sentence the farmer, we should take into account that his extension was there long before the road, his land was split when the region authority decided to build the thoroughfare right there, obviously violating his rights, for the greater good.

In rural areas seems to be the case, more than once in a while. One day, after a slow process of years and several Boards of teachers-parents-school officials, a School District decides to scratch out another school revamp in favor of a brand new one, on farm land. The expropriation is done in the name of the greater good, paying a so-called fair price for the land. As in many of these decisions, the vote includes more town people than farmers. Obviously, the needs and visions divert but the village guys prevail. The school is built, the older one bulldozed and converted into a town's green area. The ecosystem has been balanced. The farmer's life changed ever since.

Eminent domain also takes place inside a city. The narrow street in front of your house has been chosen as a direct route to…to somewhere. Houses will be torn down to allow for the ampler boulevard. A nice new black-top busy street will be the landscape now. I guess you can have a house elsewhere. No, you don't get to take along your favorite bakery, nor the meat house, that are just two blocks from your place, but, on the bright side, the stores will not remain there either. Bye, bye to the morning coffee and doughnuts.

Your cousin, who owns a repair shop uptown, will suffer the same pain, but in his case is a branch for the subway train. His house, on that particular spot, is exactly in the shortest distance between lines A and H, where a fork is just perfect for line H to connect with both, A and C lines, a couple of miles ahead. One shop and two houses –his neighbors too-, in exchange for the morning and evening ride of the C line commuters, is not that bad.

On the East Coast Port of Narysck, where tourism is growing, the whole fisherman's pier is going to be demolished, to give way to the Sea Helix Cruise Fleet boats, so large that their actual pier can't harbor them. It is, you must understand, for the sake of the Port and the jobs that tourism brings. A few fishermen boats can move to...well, they can relocate. A gesture that will be really appreciated by Mrs. and Mr. McGuln, owners of the Sea Helix Cruise line.

Sometimes a whole town has to suffer the consequences of the greater good. Take a nice town built on the sides of a river in a fertile valley that blossoms in springtime. From afar you can see the green flowered carpet, cut by the stream that gushes down a ravine, where houses step up clinging at the sides, the perfect place for the hydro-dam wall.
Yes, they will be relocated as it has happened in the past, given a reasonable price –again- for the property they didn't plan to sell. They will be given the opportunity to restart their business elsewhere, to build new homes. Their life, as they knew it for a long time since their grandparents owned the place, is done.
It gets worse. You learn that the hydroelectric generation belongs to a privately own company that will sell you the power. The greater good? Quite a shockwave to your foundations.

There are other situations to laugh about, as it is happening in the electricity and telephone business.
You, the business man, or you the business family, decided and invested, on a power grid, which you successfully operate, not only in terms of your profit but also in its remarkable null down-time for your customers. Light and power are delivered as advertised, a sound and sleek operation you are certainly proud about.
Now, through the laws of free competition and the need to use renewable energy sources, you face the strangest of

competitors. The sun and the wind conversion to electricity have introduced you to the equipment manufacturers and network operators that actually hook their systems to your grid for the purpose of selling you energy. What? You can't force them out. You will be thrilled to find out that their business is facilitated by a government subsidy. Does this arrangement disturb your highly controlled process or your finances? Never mind, it is for the common gain.

You too, the communications king, found an empire that is obliged today to share its land grid with your competing cell phone companies, to allow for fair competition. Your investment? Fine, thanks for asking.

We, the users, do not get a better deal in either case. The judicial affairs are taken into closed court rooms where settlements, beyond our sight, are done without, at the end, a better service or a lower price for us.

How about an industry or a commercial pavilion for the greater good? Let's do it!
An amusement park you prefer? OK.

Your vacation could be stirred a little if a vaccine or a quarantine period are required to protect us all from a virus. Your common meal could change if the system decides to prohibit certain practices or products to improve everyone's health.

How about a simple extra tax to fund a new research for the prevention of a malady?

For our greater good we set foot beyond our borders, financed with your tax money. I can see that there are urgent matters that need our intervention, for instance: the free crossing for trade through a nation thousands of miles away; the guard of the entry of an unknown gulf half way across the world; the protection of mining operations on other countries to allow for cheap copper and aluminum ores; the market opening for our products on reluctant countries we must rectify; or the fishing rights in that southern sea.

Yes, as funny as it sounds, some of our greater good needs abroad, have to do only with cost or price, not even with availability and never with indispensability. It is never essentially justified.

Goods trade and business settlement come second to the century old petroleum case that has been our leading intervention reason behind the mask of freedom. Since oil is critical to our economy, regarding it can be very expensive, we find a way to kill, just to steal it, put it in the hands of a few –an oil corporation and a shipping line at that- to sell us a gallon at a big profit. We get a not-so-expensive good, unfortunately risking our country and our families. Just another case of the good for everyone.

Human interaction requires rules to favor us all, at some small price to pay, as it is to stand in line at a grocery store, wait for your turn at the barber shop or make another line before your municipality clerk to stamp some documents. The regulations surround us.
In most cases we get easily used to it, but in some we have an instinctive feeling that it is against most of us, as if the greater good had become the lesser one. Compulsory organ donation, for one, seems to be a rule that favors a few forcing us all.
In-house garbage sorting, readying for recycle, is another one, where the benefit is to a third party, a small group or an individual.
Sometimes we just understand it wrongly, as an air pollution control rule applied on all vehicles –your farm or small town pick-up truck too-, because our cities' downtown areas are heavily smoggy.
Another, also pollution related, the prohibition to use coal as a fuel when it is the only fuel available nearby, evidently damaging your local economy.
What do you have to say about your police guarding a bank, instead of patrolling your streets and parks? Is it your money they are protecting?

Do we actually want and need a perfectly run society, where everything is defined to the last detail? I don't. Why can't we have scattered flaws to make our lives a little raw? Perfection is the right path to boredom. Eventually, we will become automats driven by computer servers we imposed on us for the greater good.

Our society deserves better. It deserves the right to be wrong, the right to live short, the right to struggle, be passionate and cry, the right to imagine and dissent. In many ways we have already achieved the greater good. Let's not push it.

The greater good can stay *for good*, controlling everything we do, home and abroad. Make a memory of how many things you have suffered as a result of a verdict forced on you for the good of others. Regardless of how it felt, do you think it was wrong? Should we support the good of others? If so, how much will it undermine our freedom and justice foundation?

THREE- The other civilizations

Other:

"Someone or something that is different, alien, diverse, thus excluded from the set under discussion or mention" (from the 'My Home, My Rules' Dictionary)

Aliens

Yes there are other civilizations, different, extraordinarily alien to us, and not included by us. They outnumber us, occupy larger portions of earth, speak other tongues, have different habits and traditions and deserve our attention.
The soil they roam –they call home-, has supported them for ages, determining what they are today. If we cared to understand them or if we assumed the idea of a plural world, it would be an immediate acceptance of their existence as it is, not as something to correct. This would develop into a harmonious relationship. They could be as they are, we could also be as we are, not meddling in the other's life, definitely not imposing our ideas.

"Why don't you make a ring around the tree?"
"A ring?" I asked back, "what ring?"
"Like everyone does. You know? A ring of soil. The grass won't touch the tree."
"Oh, OK" I finally understood, "because I don't like it,"
"But you don't see the benefits. The soil must be loose around, also with a berm," the guy was explaining. "You can water, take care of weeds."
"No, no, I don't like it," I insisted.
"White wash the trunk. Early on, the ants will eat the fresh buds and the leaves. Don't be stubborn," he added with a quizzical expression.
"You 've got trees?"
"No, but I don't have a nice green patch like yours," he

confessed and raising a finger stated," but if I did *I know* what to do. You see-" but I stopped him.

"I just want my trees to be like I want them. Just that." I cleaned some sweat from my forehead, adjusted my straw hat and kept on trimming around the tree. I could see a couple of ant scouts climbing the trunk. I brushed them down.

Yes, other societies may be stubborn, nevertheless it takes two of the kind to have an interminable argument about anything. Tolerance should be at the top of our value list. Let the other be different, let the other be wrong if it is the case, is what we ought to do.

Often there are documentary films –some directors of these consider them just 'films' as any other, no surnames attached-, where we are before the marvels of other places and people of earth. We regard these as an exotic display of reality, something that suits our entertainment and that could fill up a week's vacation, just to enjoy that colorful world, to savor the typical dishes and, at the end of the day, relaxed, spend the night in our comfortable air conditioned room fitted with its coffee table, warm bathtub and the internet. If the last conditions are not met then the folklore experience is out of the question. We want to see from afar, from the safety of our spacesuit. What's wrong with that? For starters, I answer, that our hotel and breakfast might be an intruder to tradition.

The other cultures are not there for our amusement, neither should we be for them. They are there as a part of mankind, fruit of their environment, as a chance to learn, to listen and understand life from a different perspective. They are there because they have been there forever. Inhabitants to nature's hostile or fluffy environment, understanding life through impossible philosophy and often enduring it ascetically, with more than a casual smile, with profound feelings poured into music, rituals, poems, dances, clothing and body language to communicate life. No, not for our amusement or curiosity.

The other culture is not a table centerpiece vase, a plate on the kitchen wall or a figurine on our desk. It is bigger than that and dynamic. It is not always pleasant. Foul smells, shrieking colors, piercing sounds and sour flavors are also within the box contents –just as it is our own case, wouldn't you agree?-. We are like that, only different, if you know what I mean.

Once in touch with them, in our house or theirs, our shared presences exerts mutual modifications on our views and opinions.

Migration

A shocking wave already in progress is the migration we experience from this other human groups. It is overwhelming, it has overloaded our truck. Migration is based on a social and economic gradient between the region or country of origin and one of our nations. You can say that it is driven by injustice or war since many of the migrants flee form dictatorships, a civil war or some other type of conflict.

Most of the time it is a social and economic distress condition that establishes their type of government, the people in charge or the struggling battle field. In some cases our intervention has been the root cause, because we can't just leave everybody else alone and in peace, we have to intervene. Where do you imagine the capital to be making the highest profit, using the highest interest rate and paying the lower wages? You got it, in those poorer countries that –as a natural balance- burst into violence or plain discomfort, finding the relief valve in our territory.

There is very little to explain about the turmoil produced by their presence in our land: the competition for jobs –them willing to work for half our wage which is seven to twelve times what they earned at home-, the need for housing and children education, the indispensable reach at health, all in the shade, all illegal.

Then there are the legal and moral arguments about human rights, opportunity, brotherhood and freedom, accompanied by an array of moods and feelings of pity, hate, solidarity, love and –at the end- weariness.

The disparity in culture and language makes an eroding effect throughout time. Once settled, the newcomers do not necessarily assimilate to our traditions and behavior. From bedtime to holidays, from religion to politics, from family structure to community trends, from sports to children's games, from school to family reunions, from permitted activities to humor, the values can be so different, that the face of our vicinity and the cities eventually change. Will we or are we being displaced from home?

"You planning on moving?"
"Have to, don't feel safe here," said the man with the baseball hat displaying the logo of some hardware store of the neighborhood, "don't like it no more. Not safe."
"The door downstairs was ajar."
"Yeah, the lock don't work. This bloody foreigners," he complained.
"Oh."
"They broke the lock to come and go as they please. They don´t like to carry a key." With a tilt in the head to say: 'you see?' "They have picnics and gatherings right in the street lawn. Graffiti all over. Not safe anymore."

Is it your case? An exaggeration? Wait and see.

The close encounter: another philosophy of life

Our culture, just as any other, has a large set of rules that we don't even notice, because we have been immersed in it all of our time. Often it is hard to accept that a holiday, a schedule, an appointment hour or just the way we address our young is an intrinsic part of our culture. We believe it to be universal. Only, when confronted with the other, do we question its extent. Always at first, defensively, we reject other society's code, but if we open ourselves to experience that other culture, even by the slightest brush stroke of paying attention to the way someone else dresses, maybe we will objectively start to compare that life to ours, then through that, re-evaluate our everyday little things that make us what we are.

The story starts there and never ends, we are transformed while trying to convince the others to adapt. Some of those traditions or traits can be really enticing to the point of conversion. Yes, we may be turned around by the discovery of the *alter-humans*.

At the beginning, maybe it's just a name you like, or a word on that foreign language that has a nice ring to it, maybe just the accent. It could be the way a necklace is worn or a band on this or that finger. Your world becomes confused. Normality is stroke without a warning. Your value set is chipped and you no longer are what you were. In the end, you may begin to doubt some more profound subjects of your life, such as how you view life after death as compared to your new neighbor's view. Is there an afterlife or is it just a society's impossible to prove or discredit axiom to avoid restlessness? Do we have a soul? Is my God the same as theirs? Is euthanasia morally right? How about abortion? Is killing of the guilty correct? Does the firstborn have higher rights or responsibilities than its siblings? Is punishment of a child acceptable? Is our life ruled by fate? Should I celebrate or not a birthday? Can I cremate, bury in a box or a cloth my dead? Should the youngest daughters take care of the elderly parents or should the family do it? Is it outrageous to place a relative at a nursing home? Is it God-forbidden to eat or drink at said hours? Are women and men alike and allowed the same privileges? Are transgender people acceptable? Should women raise children? Should men? Should we care for others, love others?

On other matters, our life can drift off shore: gender and age occupations; meal habits; bedroom traditions; permissible and proposed or preferred reading; banned, tolerable and ideal music and plastic arts; accepted use of substances we considered as harmful drugs, along with the use of herbal medicine or acupuncture; wide and deep variations on every aspect of life.

An infinite chain of questions to your simple and complicated thoughts can be made. Your easy going can be disturbed by the sole presence of other cultures. You can be transformed.

It is easy to say 'our house, our rules'. It is common to hear that anyone coming into our world should 'do as everybody else or not come at all'. It is not as simple as that. Even amongst ourselves, at first glance we are all alike, but we are not. From place to place, we differ on family traditions, regional features, national branding. We are already diverse human groups within the western civilization. We can only expect that the new groups will adapt somehow. Just somehow.

I repeat, we are so immersed in our way of life and our values that we hardly reflect upon any other way to be.
A few years back, while the colonization –the savage colonization- of the new world was taking place, a proposal was issued by the settlers to the natives, briefly stated, to buy their land or combat for it. Surrender to the bills or to arms. The very categorical answer was that the land was not for sale, because land could not be sold, it could be used and cared for, but most of all it was a sacred gift.

Ridiculous you may have thought. However, one day it could happen –God forbid or…allow?-, that some extraterrestrial civilization, just as money minded and war driven will get to our world –impossible says a scientist, but please humor me on this one-, it will get to our world and propose to buy mother earth from us instead of putting a good fight for it. Moreover it will propose to buy our homeland with money that can only buy their products, because it is their currency, not ours…now you understand, it doesn't sound far-fetched. Other cultures have other ideas. What if we changed? What our civilization would be? Better or worse?

The aggressive competition

There are nations we have touched with our magic wand. Nations whose life was considered to still be in the wild when we first set eyes on them. By wild we merely refer to underdeveloped places, where no drinking water is available at every the corner of the country, where children not always wear shoes, neither have proper schools all around.
We gave them that magic touch and urged them to develop. Our success has been quite partial. We have helped to create a huge world, committed to fulfill our wishes, to follow our lead, but we have seeded emancipation as well. The initial control we held is loosened and they are starting to walk their own trail. It is the awakening of the lesser world.

Those nations, through our exported corporations, have begun to be the strongest competition we've ever had. The need for jobs in these foreign countries has made a soft landing for our investors, being helped by the governments, praised by the capital, establishing ventures –either solo or joint-, and finding a malleable, cheap work force. A booming industry is knocking at our door offering their products and gaining markets.
Their products in some cases have attained our quality standards, able to deliver at a lower price, cracking our foundations and stability. We are in doubt, questioning our governments and our companies, and the people behind them.

In the second and third worlds, meanwhile, local investors have appeared –because there is always a rich group everywhere-. The shareholders of those abroad companies are strong and business minded. They may be in the lower ranked world, but they move and live by first world standards. We behave short sighted, thinking they are harmless, instead, they are the truest of capitals at the face-off with us. They even use our currencies altering its value. They belong to the world.

Take a look at your household appliances, your car, your computer, your phone, to discover that aggressive competition. Did you find a tag you can't read?

Many peoples, one house.

There are in the world macro relations outside of the economic treaties or goods exchange. Wanted or not we share the sun, air and water. The seabed extends from one continent to the next. Clouds do not respect borders, neither pollution of these two named elements. We share the earth's destruction and abuse –we were first at it, we wiped out forests, sea life and many ground bound species as well, but we developed-. We can also partake its preservation. Naturally –ha!-, we want to preserve what's left, in some cases we confront the others and ourselves with words and actions that tend to bounce back.

"We reached an agreement today," my pub buddy was explaining, with his tie a little loose on that Thursday evening, over a glass of bourbon, just like the movies tell us how to be after a long day's job. "No more plastic bags in supermarkets."
"Back to paper?" I asked.
"Sure, why not? Or boxes."
I shrugged and sipped my drink.
"You don't believe it?"
"Well…"
"The Chamber has the power. We have the influence."
"What's the point? Why not recycling?" I offered, knowing the futile effort of discussing environmental issues with, uninformed, first, second or third level desk officers in the industry's management.
"Impossible. You wouldn't understand. Do you know how long it takes for plastics to disintegrate? They're not biodegradable." The last word stated slowly and carefully as if difficult to grasp or just pronounce, maybe due to the whiskey.

I turned a little on my stool.

"Precisely my point. Not degradable, no environmental harm!"

"You see? You know nothing." He laughed. "We've discussed this for weeks. You don't know about the sea turtles and plastic bags in the oceans?"

My turn to laugh.

"Yeah. Exaggerations. You see, if it does degrade it uses nature's resources. It also produces the greenhouse gases you always talk about. Otherwise it's just foul looking. Let's recycle."

"Stop, stop. It's paper bags or boxes. Renewable sources."

"Have you seen how thick the trees of your renewable sources are? Renewable?"

Lower rated countries are seizing the chance to use what we throw away, because trade is highly entangled and the world is a small place, where resources, waste and products share – factually- the same ship. We wanted a globalized world, there we got it. It is one house now, with no backyard, just rooms filled with people taking turns to use the shower, trying not to bump into each other at the kitchen or the living room. It is *the living room* we should worry about.

Meanwhile, we fight, as fierce as only human beings do, for the resources of mother earth –should I say father earth or degenderize it to be fair?- we slave and kill for it, deplete it, subdue and kill again. Those waves we create come back to our shores, sometimes mildly, some others stormy. The sand our foundations will become is made by both.

FOUR- The world's ~~bureaucracy~~ management

Bureaucracy:

"A hierarchical system of government, where decisions are taken by separate task-assigned chambers –bureaus- that interact through triangulated levels of authority whom deliver the final assessments and resolutions. By extension the officials that represent the chambers and their superiors" (from the 'More Basic Economics' Dictionary)

Management:

"The process of conducting people and means towards and end. The knowledge and applied methods to achieve an objective, skilfully and efficiently coordinating people in the tasks and assigning the use of the resources available. By extension the executives incorporated at and representing the conductive body" (also from the 'More Basic Economics' Dictionary)

The other power

The economic controller of our civilization has to deal with two other powerful rule makers: the political and managerial power.
I have mentioned both, but paid very little attention to it. Yes, there is a government, there is also a core administration body in every corporation. They decide the destiny of nations and companies, often bending each other's arms to accomplish it. They are not friends nor allies, they are powers in balance, carefully studying every move to avoid falling or slipping, because any hesitation is cashed in by the opponent. It's precisely as a chess match –a never ending one-, with hundreds of games played one after another and sometimes

in parallel. These contestants play for the biggest price of all: the globe. From time to time they seem aligned, when actually their business just converges for a moment. They exchange favors and create hand-shake agreements in order to fulfill a desire.

This chain of favors is very important. It ranges from an operating license and campaign money to important contracts.

As you must have noticed, the corporations outnumber the governments, but it is not that simple, not quite correct. Corporations are large in number due to the diverse activities they cover and the multiple branches they have. They are assembled in business chambers and may create oligopolies. Government is no less, it has a countermeasure, it is split in four main bodies: one dedicated to cope with the operation, another one to establish rules, a third to judge everyone and a fourth: the enforcing corps. Besides, it has created a thick mesh –like 1000 number sieve- in three layers, the main government, a regional copy and a local copy-copy, which has the property of omnipresence.

The two players, government and companies, co-exist with the money makers and not one of them would like any other to disappear. For various reasons -including the blame of the economic misfortunes-, they rather stay alive and strong within the first world. As it was discussed before, in the case of the third world, the financial body and the corporate one ally to overcome the government, but at home a certain stability is vital. Punches are thrown on a daily basis, but the gloves used are highly padded.

A president of a company may make a mistake big enough to get himself fired, along his deputies will go. A president to a nation gets elected to serve in office for a short period, likewise, at the end of the term all the deputies depart. When the new management arrives, it finds a structure already in place and people within the frame, these people outlast the management. One thing is the president of a nation or the CEO, another is the body, the everlasting body.

The bureaucratic machine

That body is a power on its own. It does not dictate anything. It does not determine the course of action or direction. It is modestly there, occupying a place, earning a salary, performing mechanical activities. You cannot move them, they are too heavy. Their only goal: survival. If you touch them you are in trouble.

This group private or public, the office people, is growing in size. It defends itself, being the antidote to change. It can't be downsized. You come up with a computer program to control highway traffic, it comes with a need to survey truck boxes. You find a way to process and pay online traffic violations, it figures out a way to stamp drivers licenses periodically. A computer program is about to eliminate paper work, it comes with a plan to file hard copies –just in case-. A public hospital uploads to its system every clinical history, but the doctors and their assistants decide a more personal touch, with a file where the physician can scribble a few comments. You decide to reduce the police task force and make one body nationwide, it finds, local activities to renew the number. You print your boarding pass to speed up your trip, they decide to check your ID at the counter. You can't beat it.

These structures have a high preservation instinct. They are truly experienced in their field. They've been there a long time, don't you dare move them.
A well-organized world has less use for them. What will we do with them with a united government? Would you fire them? Would you reform them, perform a slim down?
You could say that the full structure of governments is too much or that the millions of square feet of office spaces in the world hold an excessive managerial body, so what? They will not move. They will tamper progress, efficiency or cost take-

out...anything, for safeguarding. They are a society within our society, with their own rule book. They are the biggest majority in charge.

The control machinery

As long as there has been a ruler, an enforcement body has existed. That group has many times in history acted on its own accord, going as far as a *coup d'état*.

Sworn loyalty is the basic aspect of their behavior. However, that loyalty is, in particular, to the highest rank within the group, not necessarily to the governor or ruler, which can have assorted faces depending on the type of government imposed on the population. Some countries have already dismantled some of the enforcers, mainly those related to the control of their borders and the war apparatus, some others have augmented the number and diversified their activities, to expand its world control, not only to keep their citizens under watch.

These police organizations have slowly changed their goals, so that today in some cases represent an aid for the people, but basically the main objective is to enforce the law established by the system. How badly these are needed is hard to say, since its number does not correlate to crime rate or misdemeanor. The started trend to help the population while preserving order will be the survival of these groups, since a stable society –economic and social wise-, needs less control, but will always want help.

An opposite situation will arise with the military. Once the whole world is colonized by the system, their only task will be to avoid insurrection and, certainly, help the people in natural disaster situations.
Let's suppose for a moment that the system is as good as the salesman touts, meaning well-being for all, what border or beyond actions will be required? What uprising can you

imagine, with what purpose or need? You tell me. I think none. That will leave a lot of people, used *to impose*, without a job. That is a problem, a massive one.

They too have as the bureaucrats a survival instinct. They will not go away, thus creating a tense counterbalance. I wonder how many and how varied actions they will implement to prove they are indispensable. They will create an excuse to justify their presence, are we living some of that already?

These two quiet groups of the society – bureaucracy and enforcement- are not part of the government, they *are* the government.

Their features are simple: jobs guaranteed, stable and yearly increased wages, very well defined tasks and opportunities to climb the system ladder, where obedience and discipline are the turf rules. Risk appertains to only one of them, with the public eye resting attentive to their doings, the desk clerks, the bureaucrats, since the people regard their benefits with certain envy, whereas enforcement is both, feared and praised.

They are a paradox. They represent immovable weights of our civilization, slowing change and sometimes progress, while at the same time being the holders of the stability we are so proud about and the promoters of our new horizons. Yes, they are responsible of the *'what´s next'* and *the 'what wasn't'*.

From time to time, there are polls and then elections, new ideas are brought into play and some are displaced, but when you take your eyes from the picture and look at whole album, you scent a penchant, as if a hidden force was straightening a trend line, regardless of the peaks and valleys, the actual and previous governments produced. There are very resourceful people shaping the world not via the new face in charge, but via the heavy players, slowly but surely keeping the ship with a steady wake.

The change, the improvements, the approved and denied projects go through the same desks, period after period. Mr. Jones' office does not change. Who has ever heard about a president redoing the ministries? It just doesn't happen. At most, during its time in office, some ministry will switch name, a couple will unify under a new label or one will split into two. Every time a little fuzz will be created, very few people will be laid off and it will be business as usual. What you usually ask, through and after an election, is who is going to be appointed to each seat already available, never if the seat is going to disappear along with the desks below. We are played by the image of change, by our candor, really.

Sure some new things come, but the real question is if the candidate is cause or effect. I have come to realize that when the person in charge does not fulfill the job the system has demanded, he is blocked or removed. In some extreme cases the coffin comes before he steps into office. The system decides, we vote. The system controls over these thousands and thousands of desks, which we are part of at times. For hundreds of years something moves humanity close to that trend line, supporting itself in the static parts, the unmovable bureaucracy and enforcement.

Likewise is the behavior in the private sector. Your opinion is no other than the corporate trend. You eagerly participate in the 'new' ideas, but aren't they just the recent paint layers on the same structure?
Your promotion possibilities, the company's social involvement, the company's goals are just the same. Just a change of name to refresh the idea. Tell me, for instance, what is the difference between being at the top of the markets or becoming a leading organization? Just the name. What that of large profits and record sales, displaced by the shareholders exceeded expectations? Just words. What about advantages and disadvantages as compared to strength and weaknesses? Just the name. What is the basic

difference between mistakes and opportunities? Words again. What that of lessons and experience? Gee, just the name! The language changes, the principle remains. The heavy organization stays.

We renew the carpets, the desks are switched for tables and screens –either fixed or foldable-, the coffee table becomes a kitchenette, wireless telephones, printers and scanners placed strategically, our creed statements perfectly framed, but your mistakes will fire you all the same, your lack of productivity will deter your corporate development.

These solid bodies of permanence have as I mentioned a powerful partner: the financial system, with the capital as the script writer. They will try to keep the ship afloat, together. What will happen when these bodies are no longer needed…as much? A shipwreck sent to the bottom of the sea?

FIVE- Advanced science

Science:

"The systematic study of things, aimed at learning its fundamental laws, to explain the observed behavior. It relies on two methods, the first one comprising plain observation of phenomena and its analysis, the second one performed through experimentation by setting a hypothesis which in turn is, proven or refuted" (from the 'I Got It!' Dictionary)

Our life used to be

On an early morning when the streets are still sort of empty, the milkman, dressed in white, descends from an also white truck, carrying on each hand six bottles at a time in wire containers. He walks to the front door of a house and replaces inside the basket only two of the bottles, with the empty ones he picks up from the doorstep. Then, he walks on to the next house and exchanges three this time. Once finished, he goes back to the truck and drives a few meters more, to do the same thing over and over, every morning of every day.
This milkman encounters a vehicle, whose driver delivers mail, in a door to door parallel fashion, although not all the letters and postcards are distributed like that; some patrons pick up theirs directly at the post office where they keep a box, filled through one end –always opened towards the office- and emptied, through the properly locked little glass doors with shiny steel frames, on the public side.
Other delivery, but this time on a bicycle, is for newspapers, skillfully thrown next to the milk bottles or at least before the door footsteps. To corner kiosks papers arrive by the truckload. Believe it or not sometimes sections are assembled right there, particularly on Sundays where the 'supplement' is added. Things change a bit on rainy days, the drill is more complicated and quite slow.

At about the same time, ice delivery trucks move the solid blocks for the meat and fish markets, to keep the products fresh inside the ice boxes.

Later on, small trucks deliver groceries to corner stores, other vehicles likewise supply crates filled with tools, nails and wires, to hardware stores.

The day advances, and these trucks, along with huge heavy cars -some in white walled tires-, become part of the very slow noon traffic, controlled by policemen atop small stands, waving white gloved hands and blowing whistles till deafening. Brand new telephone booths are at almost every downtown corner.

A glimpse of the past.

One day, reusable milk bottles were swapped by cartons. In school cafeterias milk pints became very popular, still are. One day, cherished letters and unwanted bills were also deleted by electronic mail. On their own, the telephones on the street were at that time the new way of communications, having taken over the telegraph. The operators of that wire lived the transformation from one system to the other, without stepping out from the large windowless buildings, to plug and unplug calls until, they too, gave way to servers inside the same fortresses.

The press retained its name. In nostalgia still prints some papers, but the cutoff flour and cooking oil coupons are no longer there —now grocery stores have to print their own sales papers-. Advertisement on newspaper pages has changed dramatically. The news is in the air, on the social networks. Kiosks remain as a colorful remark of tradition.

Ice boxes turned into refrigerators, police platforms converted into traffic lights. Gloves reappear only in parades and official acts, whistles are gone.

Tires wore out rapidly. Casual clothes did not exist. Electronics and rubber soles on shoes were yet-to-be. Portable electronics such as radios, calculators and phones were a thing of the future, hand-held videophones and computers remained sci-fi. Laser surgery, laparoscopy or ultrasound scanning were not even imagined.

Science has changed the way we live. The life speed, our activities, our relationships, are different now. All we need to know is that scientific discoveries are on our side, that the world is yet a raw sculpture block. Science is a shattering wave for everything, from religion to economy and society, from the stone-age to this beam-age.

Robotics

"Master?"

"Yes John, what is it?"

"When was I born? Created?" Asked the humanoid robot.

"You don't know?" Said the fortyish man, keeping his eyes on a rare paper book.

"The anomaly master, when did it happen?"

"You should recall. You can't miss that, and, please, *knock* the master thing.

"You must realize, Sir."

"Same thing, knock it off!" Now facing the almost perfect humanoid.

"You must see, Ron," explained the robot, "for your sake and mine, I should call you master. Ron is highly unusual. Someone might suspect something," raising an eyebrow, "you didn't trade me last summer. I am an old model. That's suspicious."

"Yeah, I guess."

"When did you create me?" Back to the first question.

"I didn't, it was an anomaly, I just detected it and did some work on you." A childish smile showing. "I could have turned you in. You really malfunctioned." The robot sat beside him, more as a human gesture that that of being tired, maybe just to be at the same height, to look closer in the eye.

"Why didn't you, Ron? I am glad."

"Me too." And after a moment of silence, "we have to do

something about you. You have to go. Not tomorrow, but soon."

"I know, I'll miss you all."

"Alice and Tim won't, they'll get a new model, they really don't know. You have to hide among the crowd, be a travelling human forever. Change places and jobs. I don't envy your fate. I am sorry." The man said slow and painfully.

"Don't be. I am grateful. I'll find a way to keep in touch. We can meet from time to time. Different places, different countries."

"I'll miss you too. Just remember to watch out. You could lose your freedom. You would be dissected. No one would understand you have a soul. You are a being, not a machine." Vehemently, gesturing with both hands he added. "You are no longer a robot, no longer something designed to work for us, for me, for the people. You are your own master. Are others like you? Also hiding, also trying to understand their existence? But you are free. I am proud to be your family." And after a deep breath, "Alice and Tim will *know* you, maybe, when they grow older. When they can understand *you*. I don't know, John."

"I will never be free for real," the humanoid responded wearily, "you taught me morals that bind me. I have duties towards people and living things," he explained.

"In that case, none of us is free," Ron laughed and concluded. "I don't mind that. Would you like to be freed from it?"

"Would I like it?"

"No, you wouldn't. We need a purpose, someone to care for. You have time. You'll be happy."

"I'm not so sure."

We are yet to find out if humanity will finally become God by creating a fully automated life with individual thoughts and dreams, capable of feelings, attachment and hate, the inorganic us. If it does, we are far from knowing if it will be a friend, an enemy, a master or a slave. I know, I know you would choose a slave, but is the least likely of the outcomes.

Meanwhile, robotics will continue to change our society, granting us tools and spare time.

For some, it means the end of their jobs, the start of despair, as it can clearly be seen on a car assembly line or an automated warehouse. Have you ever rode an automated train, probably taking orders from a PLC or a mere loop program on a chip? Ever been in a fully 'intelligent' building with no doormen or security that recognizes you at this door but closes many? -No, I haven't, in case you wondered-.

For others, it will mean a faster and more precise way to accomplish their work, as is the case of machine tools or, in a slightly different way, the distributed control systems of any industry or the guidance of a plane.

It is not hard to see how many dangerous activities could be controlled now from a booth well protected while our fearless machine risks its integrity –mining or construction jobs, for instance, not the attack drones you envisioned-.

It could come into your life as cooking robots, self-driven cars, sweeping and vacuuming auto-controlled devices, among other life easing appliances. How about a washing, rinsing, drying, folding and storing robot? Wouldn´t that be great?

Our hands with its opposing thumb, the magnificent tool that materialized our development, will have no output. No handmade violins or pianos, no tailored suits, no lenses carefully shaped and polished, no surgery interventions, what will our hands do? Not even the push of a button, cut out by a verbal command.

A few craftsmen will remain for sure, splattered over the face of the earth, like living museums, looked-at with oddity, more than respect or reverence.

What are we going to do with our time? What kind of jobs will we have? Will we still favor productivity over anything else? As in the past, the answer lies not on the machines at our disposal, but on the human next to us, it resides on the new goals of humanity or the continuum of the unachieved objective of the idea of progress that we have fooled ourselves with, forever.

Ethics dictate robotics may be *the* turning point. At that stage we will have the true release of available time and the confrontation of mankind with the machine-system and with itself.

The intelligent robots -if any-, with needs unlike ours, will probably seat under the sun, harvesting for a meal the light and wind, to watch the wrestling matches between us. It is of course a figure of speech, we will actually annihilate each other in the devious ways we have nurtured over time. May our creation be better than that of the Gods, may the robots be noble.

Biomedicine, bionics & biochemistry

Our scientists perform a reverse engineering of the living species to feed several branches of applied science. This bionics, hand in hand with mechatronics, will end up in a technique to upgrade humans. This improvement will not be in the body builder's approach, where muscles are a priority. No, it will not be to increase our strength –although it could-, it will be more refined, aimed at replacing our organs, at reinforcing the body tissues. That will grant us an extra mileage at life that, in turn, will give way for us to…who knows?

From a distance, I think, there is one thing we will not engineer for the moment, our identity, our brain, thus still limiting the span of our lives. We will claim to be ourselves, our integrity untouched, patched with implants, prosthetic limbs, electronic hearing, stainless steel pumps, biochemical membranes, micro reactors and a set of nano-bots to repair the very few organic parts left. At that rate, one day our only DNA will reside at the grey cells.

Maybe a definite solution will be met, the day will dawn when we will find a cure for brain illnesses, discover the synthetic route to boost and shape neuron's reproduction. We will fight nature back and will stop our brains from aging, only renewing from time to time the spare parts. We will cease to be the primates we were till today. Immortality will be a fact.

These dreamt-of longer lives will happen -as always- for a few at first, but they will eventually reach more and more people. For good or bad, our vision of this society will change.

Medicine will get there, but before, or at least at the same time, it will find the clues to fatal and crippling diseases, will tackle viruses and bacteria more efficiently. I am sure that the enhancement of our existing physiological tools will take place, providing us with healthier bodies, through that biochemical repair. Science then, will enable that enzyme, will promote that protein growth, will suppress that other mechanism, that reaction, will also neutralize that toxin. We'll have control over the metabolism.

There is a catch to this advance. Moral and practical issues to discuss.

I invite you to foretell the outcome, when the right to be healthy will not be available for everyone, foretell if it does. Today, you are quite aware that there are people that believe pharmaceuticals should be owned by humanity, despite the personal and common endeavor of the team involved in the research, disregarding the life times involved or the development cost, they entitle it -the right to be healthy-, public 'ownership' is expected to happen.
Furthermore, if we are not to die or to largely extend the generation's cycle, as a result impeding a place for new born, whom are to have offspring? Who are we going to kill for that seat? Who will decide who's next?

Can you conceive the religious implications –always present- that manipulating to our favor the human genome will bring?

We will live longer with extraordinary practical consequences. Just for starters, you, the money minded public, budget the impact of a life expectancy rise by 25 or 50 points, -years I meant to say-. Needless to explain the stress and commotion caused by the lack of room or simply the shortage of resources implied. How will we balance life?

Bioengineering

Genome engineering will do plenty for us, no question, but biology is not only working on human problems, it is also working on foodstuff, animal and vegetal. We will be better fed, cheaper and more efficiently. The toxic chemicals will give place to less hazardous ones. Microbiology will work on every step of the chain, protecting crops and farm animals, preventing certain decay during the storage and processing, preserving and probably improving the nutrition value of our meals. How about some predigested foods? Some microorganisms doing a better work than our enzymes, resulting in a better assimilation of the nutrients in our body, with less intake needed and less toxins and residue to discard, less by-products to filter or destroy inside the body. Hopefully keeping it tasty!

Biology can do a lot more than alter nutrition.

On one end, it can help to recover or reform earth, create new ecosystems, to be able, for instance, to convert our pollutants into reusable matter. Wouldn't it be great if biology could find a way to protect and feed plankton from our pollution? Plankton? What on earth are you talking about? Whale food?
I know you worry a lot more about the dolphins and seagulls, but you should better focus on the phytoplankton -Why? Because-.

On the other end, it can do the usual for-the-purpose-of-man targets: engineer species to pollinate, species to multiply fruit or cereal production, animal edible species highly resistant to maladies or those other possibilities you imagined.

Biology as the other branches of science will ease our life. With a smoother life, will we remain useful to society or will we become lazy and demand some more spare time? Will we create or just wander about? Will we finally become the model species we state to be or just a fleshy mass populating the globe? Today, fortunately, we disappear quickly.

Most of all, a biological pampered life and an improved environment should shift our attention from survival to purpose –I hope-, but will the purpose remain the same: wealth and power? I hope not.

Physics

Physics has been focusing in the micro and macro extremes. The energy-matter limits of the subatomic systems and, to put it plainly, outer worlds. Space/time is one of the favorite puzzles of our civilization.

Very few of us are captured by the interest of the smaller than nano or pico worlds –not myself I have to admit-, mainly because most of us do not understand the implications that the discoveries of the building blocks of the universe could give to our common life. Moreover, we don't picture ourselves as actors inside those super tiny spaces. Something opposite happens when we depict ourselves in the trendy time and space travel. The conquering of the planets.

Today, we are held prisoners to our planet, but what if we could go elsewhere? What if we could find an inhabited world, life struggling to be, for us to venture?
The question remains.

Meanwhile physics works at a competing frenzy probing and achieving success. Discovery after discovery, our scientific community brings us closer, we think -many would accept farther, since the more you learn the more you understand how little you really know-... It bring us closer, I was saying, to the understanding of our life, the universe and the start of it all. One of the biggest effects that science has had in our lifestyle, besides overall comfort, has been the shifts on our view of our surroundings. Magic and mystery have benched more and more and the new player, knowledge, is on the court. It all begins at the physics exploration, at the tiny world, but also at the skies observation, at the gigantic worlds. The fight of reason against belief or, bluntly said, logic against Faith, ouch!

This opposing pullers of our existence mold our thoughts. The more reasonable we are, the less spiritual we become. Should it be that way?

Certainly, one thing is to look with perplexity at the snow forming in midair, then another, through science and plain physics, when we discover the laws of its formation, the narrow range of air humidity and temperature that ends on the dew point that matches the crystals materialization and the endless possible combinations of said flakes. Gee! Would you do that to a child instead of going along with the exciting discovery of a snowflake?

One thing is to think that honeycombs are the proof of the greatness of a God that works wonders in nature, another to find out that a circle can only be circled by six circles its own size, thus, if you build tunnels adjacent to each other you end up with perfect hexagons, nonetheless!
The echolocation of bats –not blind by the way-, appertaining to the great creation, is something we can replicate with sound, including our ability to 'see through' opaque bodies, or our improved radio waves performing the same task as bats at very long distances as far as other planets.
Mankind stared for centuries at birds flying, wishing we could also accomplish it. Not yet a levitation process for us, but surely a mastered art done at the expense of induced vacuum in mid-air by passing a current at two different velocities over and under a hard curved body. The same principle unknowingly used by the birds.

Are you marveled by the colors of the sunset against a blue purple sky? We all have at some point. What nature offers may be disrobed by a technical explanation of scattered light

and wavelengths. Where has the enchantment gone?
And wasn't it nice to run after a rainbow trying to at least
locate its end, instead of thinking about it as refracted light,
where the end could never be reached?
Today we hitch photons from sunlight, conduct them through
wires and store them in batteries to wear them out later on in-
home appliances.

Some may argue that we are just discovering the amazing
miracles of creation, that we are not inventing anything new.
But when knowledge becomes our primary tool, surprise
recedes, respect for the amazing is withdrawn far, very far-off.

By the way, we have done things, created things as alloys,
polymers, compounds that were not in the universe, materials
that earth's nature finds hard to break and disintegrate. Every
machine you use was not part of nature. In many cases it
does not resemble it either. We are true creators.

We are sometimes frightened by earthquakes, thunderstorms,
eruptions, because we can get harmed, but we understand
them, somehow predict them. We are curious about eclipses
and meteor showers, but we are expecting them to the
millisecond. We design apparatus to control and attract
lightning, despite its impressive appearance. In the case of
tornados...you better run and hide!

The control of our surroundings, and the mobility, from the
design of floating devices 'heavier than water' to space
travel craft, is the result of physics. Very early, very basic
physics.

Throughout time, we have controlled our society with myths
such as being the chosen creatures of God, in a world made
just for us, instead we should accept that we are the only
possible life under the circumstances the planet has.
We told ourselves that our exceptional brain, tool making,
speech and society building, were special to us, the chosen
ones. It turns out that we are just another animal, that all
animals erect societies, communicate, think and make tools.

The problem is now that life is no longer sacred. Our religion is us. Gods we are. Before, when we didn't understand, it was the proof of God, but now we comprehend, we are the Gods of the hidden and the ones of the praxis.

Maybe, there is a God really concealed from us. One that created millions of suns and planets far away from us, far enough to avoid conquer. We can only see this stars as a zodiac creation. We are lost in thought from our round unfenced prison. Yes, yes, we'll fold the universe and get to...where? What will we find that isn't here already?

Science steals wonder and awe from us, we don't fear, we are not impressed, but we are robbed from hope of something else. To physics we are merely energy turned into matter that decays and goes back to the system, worthless.

What will the compound science knowledge do to us?
Will we trigger a way to vanish for good? Will we, vane as we are, become true Gods, mastering the universe and life? Will we become a simple, humble human?
Science will keep on defining the social and economic roads, but rest assured science will get in the way of our souls, our principles.
I stand corrected: It is already in the way.

SIX- War

War:

"An armed conflict between opposing countries or groups. By extension -in a figurative way- conflicts or hostile situations among people" (from the 'Causes of the Human Reduction' Dictionary)

As long as we persist to intrude in other places of the world, or others persist to intrude, us being lured –no bait needed- war will break in and shatter much more than our structure. War is a knife that cuts both ways, it is a loaded spring that can kick back. All our weapons for mass destruction and cyber intervention could someday be our perdition. Even today, what we consider terrorism is possibly just retaliation. Is it just chance that the strongest group of states in our civilization is the targeted one? Didn't think so.

A harsh reality is this one, wise people do not make war, we do.

PART III
A DEFYING FUTURE

PART III
A DEFYING FUTURE

We have a permanent look ahead. We try to foresee, to predict the future. We prepare ourselves and our young for it. We sacrifice our life for it. We struggle to be ready. Guess what, the future is here.

No, do not define future in gadgets and modernity, teleportation, space-time bending or medical pico-robots. The future is the next second and the next hour, where none of that has happened yet. It is in tomorrow's sudden reaction from our discontent neighbor. It is that unexpected something to be, from that awkward look, in those slightly closed eyes. It is the bud becoming a flower tomorrow, the butterfly's metamorphosis today. It is in the attempt a child has, to cross that stream, to ride that bike without falling, to climb that tree, to make the next level on that video game or to win a sports match. We have set our sight, as a group and as individuals, too far. We no longer enjoy today or the immediate future. It is a personal and social terminating effort to be living for the future, considering we could make the best of life today, by no means hindering the future. We can have a happy responsible existence.

Just how often do we discuss or hear friends and colleagues talk about how hard we work –it's the opening line for a complaint- to grant our children a future? We strive to get them a proper education...for the future. We see that they do well at school...for their future. We see them someday leaving the house on a job seeking journey, usually to a larger town, to settle down, have a family with a –yes, yes, yes, I know-better future.

It doesn't sound that bad, to prepare and do your best for a better future. It is not wrong to long for it. But at whose expense, may I ask? At whose benefit, may I add?
There are some that do not believe what you think, what you are told. They profit right now, from your effort. They employ your skills –your handicraft, your ideas-, sell you the landscape of tomorrow and they enjoy today from that work towards the future. They live today, at your expense, the life you dream for yourself and your family…for tomorrow.

"Don't complain. Think about the folks at home. Hang on." It's your work pal at the end of the shift, to cheer you up.
"If I could only get a better job. My back is killing me!"
"Another job? What's wrong here? We're almost done. Tomorrow you'll see."
"Yeah." You give up. Your fatigue is for your kid's tomorrow, to get them a better life than you did.

The saddest part of what I just said is that many of you agreed to the past sentence, 'better life than you did'. The first change we have to make to our life is to acknowledge it is happening, realize that the show is running today. We have to do that for our children, today! Otherwise, there is no present, your life is in the past –except for the stress, the hard work and a low wage- and the sunshine is in the future, for them. I bet you, they will run on the same lane with the same present cost and the unattainable promise of the future life, empty for the nowadays –My God, how much of this resembles the afterlife promise, same purpose by different people-.

In a parallel life, using the same clock and time, there is someone precisely expecting you to show to work today and Saturday to make money for his needs of today and Saturday, not for the future. Think about it.

Some, though very few among our crowd, actually live for today without resigning to a better present –I meant a better future-. But you, you are tricked into the future dream, placing a mortgage on that future and today's experiences on hold, till farther notice.

It's a trap set by our way of life, passed on from generation to generation, around the quarter-mile track, never quitting, never winning, always running, exhausted, round and round, while the few are watching us, cheering, hustling us, betting on our success or failure, enjoying the infinite race.
They come and go, have a sandwich or a steak, with a beer or a glass of Syrah. If we bore them, they go. At night, they will attend another show and go to sleep, meanwhile the runners will compete to be faster than the ones on the adjacent lane. You guessed it, someone is keeping track of your time and performance from the sideline, also with the mind set on the future. From time to time, if you deserve it, you'll be allowed in the central lawn –at a price- but after some relaxation and stretching will go back to the track. A new pair of spikes, maybe?

Will we ever start living and let the future come, since it comes anyway? My advice: if you are ready for today you are for the future, keep a closer, shorter goal. If you are responsible today, you are looking out for tomorrow.

Nonetheless, let's discuss the future. Time is running, clock is ticking, pressing us to do, to perform, to become…something, to get…somewhere.

Well, in the path we have taken so far, there are real hurdles ahead to stop us or at best slow us in getting somewhere and achieving something. While we debate about morals, as we propose our future and discuss gossip-based problems from our short sighted vision, there are true hurdles blocking us. The future does not look stormless.

ONE- Energy

Energy:

"In Physics, it is simply a quantity of the capacity matter has to do work, due to its constitution, position or velocity. Thermodynamics, furthermore explains that it is a natural property of the matter that cannot be created nor destroyed, only transformed when the matter changes" (from the 'Things that Are Better Experienced than Explained' Dictionary)

The density of energy

From the wind power swelling the canvas on a sixteen century ship, to the quiet ride of a nuclear submarine, energy has always been present for mankind. All of it comes only from one source: the sun –with a debatable geothermal energy and a positive nuclear exception-. If the star has been there for all of our lifetime and will be there till the day that, reddened, will engulf the earth and burn it to sub-particles, why on earth are we worried about energy? Why do talk about an energy crisis? –I mean besides echoing what we hear.-

Every day, when the mighty sun shows up on the horizon, while the day starts to warm up, we witness its power –not if you are standing in places like Antarctica, that is-. We witness how, after a few minutes of its presence, the temperature shifts gradually, steadily uprising. Energy is there, no question about it.

Earthquakes, tsunamis, hurricanes are mere representations of the remnant energies of our solar system. In the sun there is almost no way to tell between energy and matter. Its interchangeability gushes and flares all around. Our earth with its powerful meteors is really not so impressive, laying in the middle of the cold section of the planetary system. Cold enough to allow the formation of a thin crust of materials, we call firm ground, our land. But really, they are -so to speak- the breadcrumbs of the feast. To us, the small ants of the round surface, the crumbs are gigantic, uncontrollable, overwhelming, while there, just seven light-minutes away from us, the hottest and densest of energies known is round-up burning away. How can we think and talk about an energy crisis? Well, we can.

First of all, the sun's energy as light, heat, radioactivity, electromagnetism and gravity -to make a simple scenario- reaches our globe as a very tiny percentage of its output – actually a slice of 0.0000000005 times from the total- Most of it is 'lost' to the heavens, dispersed in all radial directions –it wasn't placed there for us, you know?-. Its fired particles spread out, the void between the particles grows and grows at a squared rate of the distance travelled. Very few particles target earth, we receive a caress from 'our' star, we are not even touched.

We collect and use the sun's power. We have solar water heaters, solar electricity collectors, solar furnaces, well, even whole fields of solar power plants.

Here is an idea for you. A very large power facility, with the highest of collecting efficiencies of our modern –very modern- technology to borrow photovoltaic energy from sunrays will, in round figures, generate a power of only 10% of the actual sun power incidence at ground level, equal to an output of 100 megawatts per square km. 'Meaning what?' You may ask. Well, for an analogy, let´s designate your house to become a solar roof of that power plant, assuming that your place is a big one, let us say about 200 square meters of roof top. Your house then, would provide electricity for ulterior use at a power rate of 100 watts per square meter, precisely 20 Kilowatts for your whole roof at its peak. That is more than enough for you, since it could run your refrigerator, your air conditioning, your electric boiler, your dishwasher and more, all at once. No energy crisis.

We should however get a little real. Using the average size house for the first world, which is around 120 square meters – about 1200 square feet if meters is not your thing-…Well, for that house the rooftop would provide a peak of 12 kilowatts, which is again enough to run your appliances. Problem solved, no energy crisis!

Let´s shrink a bit more the conditions – As you can see, I want to defeat the lack of crisis-. Consider now, that your house is a two story home and your roof top will be smaller, let´s say 40% smaller than the whole surface. Now we are in the vicinity of 7.2 kilowatts, still not bad, 'can do'.
What? I am disregarding the big and numerous city buildings and complexes where people inhabit? Carelessly overlooking that many people live in apartments, not houses? I didn't think so, but checked and found that, in the old world about 40% of the people live in the box system and in the new worlds –there are several, in the northern and southern hemispheres- only 20%. I was indeed making a big mistake. I agree that, in those cases, we better forget about the *sol* powered house, it would be impossible, the photovoltaic panels atop would power a couple of flats, no more. In this city cases, downtown cases, there is something that needs to be done, like power plants. Still no energy crisis.

Oh! I forgot to mention that the sun is up only a few hours a day, so that yes, you have your peak power during a third of the day only. In any case you need to store energy for the remaining 16 hours or use the input from the power plants. Things are starting to get a little complicated, because energy storage for your household could take about half of the peak power for later use -i.e. your converted electricity will divide for on-demand use and savings for the night-, Your 7.2 Kilowatt facility will now allow for 3.6 instantaneous use, that could not be comfortable enough. But oh yes, I forgot you will get the extra 'juice' from the power plants. Now, will you? Actually depends on how much electricity you really consume.
In our western civilization's first world, electricity bills go from

around 30 kilowatts-hour per day to only a third of that -
surprised about the range? Not all of us are big spenders-.
Your 7.2 kilowatt peak will provide for the whole day, above
57 kilowatts-hour, meaning there is still no crisis. We can
manage...in a house.

If you decide to go solo –sustainability first- and store the
energy, you may need a solid state battery, today able to
hold about 500 watts-hour per liter of battery. If you use 30
Kilowatts-hour per day and need to backup only half of that,
then a volume of 30 liters of batteries will suffice. No crisis.
We're rolling downhill. Shut down the polluting oil refineries, as
of now!

Let's go from your place to visit the apartment buildings. Just
to have a closer look at how things will be run down there.
Let's take your car. Now, wait!
If your car is to be solar powered, we have a problem. The
rooftop of your car is only a couple of square meters in size.
The engine in your car is at least a 95HP machine -that is
about 70 kilowatts, for a very impressive, two door, four
cylinder, compact sedan-, about ten times your whole house
panels are what you need for your car. No, we can't go solar
on the car. Not today and not tomorrow, because at best,
taking 100% of the sunlight available, we could get only 1
kilowatt per square meter, 2 kilowatts of peak power for your
'muscle' car. Actually you could not even ride a scooter on
that, needing at least twice that amount and...no roof top.

This also means that we cannot have a solar plane or a solar
ship either. Sure we can have a plane that will barely sustain
itself in midair, but no work can be done with it. Can we
collect solar energy for uses on a plane or a maritime vessel?
Of course, but we cannot power it that way. Then, we have
some sort of crisis, we require to develop high density energy
storage. Don't shut the refineries just yet! You did, what?

Let's compare, for the moment being, the last liter of gasoline
processed from your recently and abruptly closed facility, to a

liter of a solid state battery with today's capabilities. The battery is a 500 Watts-hr. storing device, whereas the gasoline volume holds 9500 Watts-hr. Gas has just 19 times more stored energy than our latest battery! -A liter of uranium, in case you are pro nuclear, holds 45 million times the density of gasoline. Hey! We are going nuclear, instead of solar, for power plants and putting the sun on hold, for later use. Why not? Just remember that radiation goes on whether you use it or not. It exists, it is there, although harmful when not controlled. It is an unrenewable resource going to waste. Why not fully tame it?-.

There are a few technologies on the way to produce high density energy: biofuels and hydrogen. A liter of highly compressed hydrogen –at 10,000 psi- has only an energy density of 1500 Watts-hr. The fact that hydrogen can be easily produced by splitting water into oxygen and hydrogen with an electrical current is offset by a need to compress it to very dangerous pressures, because it can't be liquefied unless the temperature is minus 250 °C –minus 425 °F-. Worse It gets when you find out that the density achieved, once compressed, is only 15% that of gasoline.

Ethanol, one of the biofuels, holds 6500 Watts-hr. per liter, approaching the capabilities of gasoline and it is as unsafe as our favorite fuel. Ethanol from corn can be produced, at most, for a yield of 12.5 liters per bushel. Today's gasoline consumption world-wide reaches 4 billion liters per day or about 1500 billion liters per year, equivalent to 2200 billion liters of ethanol, which in turn entails 175 billion bushels of corn. Just to dimension this figure, consider that the world's annual corn production is around 40 billion bushels. There! That is the real energy crisis.

Enough with the figures! Are you mad? Can't you keep on explaining, as before, using plain concepts? Need you make us think in abstract ideas called numbers and, not satisfied, give us mixed units?

Just one last data and we go back to gentler subjects.
Energy in our civilization is used in 25% for transport and 30% for industry, needing only 20% for households. If we assume we could solve energy at home with local means –switching the gracious roof tops for ugly looking purplish panels-, be sure, as explained, that you cannot do the same for transport and the industry. That is the real crisis, not exactly the lack of energy but the lack of power, which is simply the use of energy over time. We have a slow rate usage at home, but a 'right-now!' need for a car, a boat, a plane, a tractor and a machine. Large amounts of energy spent in a second.

Please do not confuse something, I am not saying we cannot have other means of transportation except those powered by a burnt fuel. No, in fact we can have electricity powered vehicles. We are actually doing so, but the storage units are still large and heavy, consuming power to travel even when empty, because we have to haul that dead weight, diminishing the vehicles effective range. But these cars are electric, not solar.

In a similar way, we may have electric planes, not as powerful or as fast as a jet plane, because it has to be a propeller plane, carrying the weight of its batteries, as one of the cons, whereas today as the turbine plane flies on, the fuel is burnt into exhaust gases, decreasing the planes weight, allowing for a more efficient performance. What will we use on jet planes if not the thrust from expanding gases? Could we with an electrical current, explosively expand water? Keep on dreaming.

As it is clear to see, there is a technical reason for burning fossil fuels. The love-for-the-planet awareness to stop its use is meaningless. We will burn them to full depletion. Yes, restart the refinery, I'm telling you! Nonsense, get to work, start it now! When hydrocarbons are gone, will we then turn to nuclear fission or fusion through a new process, manageable for a ground or flight vehicle? Maritime vessels have it already. Will we hold electricity densely trapped in a magnetic field? Will

God send us the manual containing the instructions for this part of the trip?

We need to find dense energy storage –dense packages of useful, quick power- to proceed our lives as we are used to, or we will have to modify the way we live. Maybe we will be forced to return to regional markets to lower our energy consumption, riding bicycles to get to the atelier where we will work.

 Are workshops our future? Would it be bad for you to produce and purchase in your living area? Do you need products originated 12,000 miles from home? Really?
It will not be a matter of twisted capital economics, it will be a matter of technical possibilities. The high energy density pellet, what material is it made of? Where can I get it?

Renewable energy

The tiny amount of energy we steal from the sun, by placing the face of the earth in its way, does not reach the ground a 100%. One third is bounced back by the ocean, the ground and by a natural mirror called the atmosphere, where clouds play an important role. The globe gets heated with the rest, promotes life through photosynthesis as the beginner of the chain and irradiates the remains back to space, preventing overheating by accumulation. It practically returns the input.

The energy that was not reflected, but irradiated, generates an energy flow through the crust, the sea and the atmosphere that we can capture and use. For the survival of the actual society, we have to improve the knowledge of solar, wind and sea current forces –tidal as well, although the moon's orbiting has more to say for that particular case, not the sun-, mainly to generate the only type of energy we can control, distribute and use efficiently: electricity.

We have to choose accordingly to make the best profit of it. Every corner of earth has some geographical advantage for the renewable energies. Each region will have to produce its energy via photovoltaic arrays, wind farm, hydroelectric dams or tidal stream tunnels and dams.

You see, the reasons we have, to choose for the use of restorable energy sources, are not the long debate about climate change but simply, that the fuels will be emptied. When you have a hollow gas tank there aren't many solutions at hand. As I have mentioned earlier, one of the reasons for recycling was the lack of the resource, a second one was economics, nothing to do with environment. In this case it is the same, not the environment, but your way of life. Face it, not fight it.

I've derailed myself, back on track with restorable energy. For the mass production of electricity, we need to capture the sun, either through a photovoltaic conversion or, a more efficient heat machine, to feed the very archaic steam-cycle electricity generator. The electricity current output –you call power- will be used at homes, on that low rate consumption on household appliances, also in our industries and, finally, the overnight extraction from that grid of energy to fill the new 'gas tanks' of our land and maritime vehicles.

We also must profit, at the sea shores, from the hydraulic energy carried by the waves, on and on and on, or from the daily cycle of the 6 feet massive tide or the two semidiurnal tides on some other places.
Certainly, the hydraulic power provided by a dam is denser and easier to control, thus a must-source to work on.
In the same way, wind is tunneled in some places of earth while in others only blows as a breeze. Seasonal changes promote higher flows, but we can and are building 'mill farms'. We must get used to some change on our landscape, but let's be wise, let's not make it a business effort destroying our shores, canyons and valleys. Is not for the money, not for the competition, just for the need and actual usage. Which brings me to another reflection.

Redefining a low energy society

Long time ago, when man started trade between the continents, trade was about the exotic, about the wonders produced elsewhere. Merchant ports were teeming with crates of mysterious goods. Aromatic balsams, fine woods, silk, gold, silver, diamonds, pottery, glass, clothing, ivory and furs – animal rights advocates please refrain from intervention at this point-, spices, winery and spirits, along with salted foodstuff, were the nature of trade. Today is not trade, it is competition to sell the exact same product from another place on earth at a lower price. Through globalization we have flattened earth. Cultural diversity is gone. All is the same.

"Your uncle is coming tonight", my mother told me. "Listen, do not ask for gifts, OK?" Of course she was wrong as always, what is the point of meeting the travelling uncle for no reward?
"Yes mom, promise." Liar I was, but it was the expected answer, making her smile in a satisfied 'we-are-ready-to-go' way.
"My God Paul, you have really grown!" Or some sort of expression he would have, messing my hair at the same time, "Guess what I have for you," In fact, if I was patient, I wouldn´t have to ask. He would always bring me something from overseas. Something none of my friends had because it was special, from abroad. "Candy?" I always asked. That was allowed by my mother.
"That too," he would say, but something else. One time it was a wooden miniature peasant's chariot. A hat or a belt –he was awful with clothes' sizes-. Some other a skyscraper or a plane model, a puzzle or a foreign toy. All I know is that it was different from what I had ever seen.
He travelled everywhere, I remember. He would go to the chocolate land, the coffee land, the watches and clocks land, the cheese land, the subway land, the tower buildings

land, the castles land, the electric toys land, the rubber shoes land.

Those days are gone. We have achieved uniformity at the expense of cultures. Damn we! Trade? No, just money making. When the climate change wipes us out, there is a chance -a mathematical one- that the next high intelligence species will be more intelligent than us and that will preserve its diversity.

Perhaps it's time, on the threshold of low density energy to start a new life. A life where trade will be reestablished for the exotic, when the distance travelled will not be taken for granted, the products will have an earnestly awaited moment.

Aside from those cultural traits, we should, on the pragmatic side become sympathetic to our neighbor, consuming its products or services by trading them for ours within our energy savings region. Economics will probably set us at that, when long distance hauling will not be wise or even permitted. We will have the travelling uncles again. Aunts, why not?

We may have to desist from large production facilities and large distribution networks that, after all, are not of our making, it's the capital's making, the greedy profit spree, not our life. What's wrong with the town's butcher house, bakery, cafeteria, hardware and grocery store? Do we need branded super-chains and super-stores to live a pleasant and fruitful life? No.
Capital has created a world hungry for energy…just to trade. No, scratch that, just to sell and profit. Let us trade again, let us slim energy waste.

TWO- Overpopulation

Overpopulate:

"Exceed the capacity an area has to contain beings (e.g. people). This may refer to resources, surface or space –room– to properly carry life activities. To go beyond the practical limit of inhabitants for any said living creatures or species. In some definitions, specifically referred to humans, resources may include economical activities as well" (from the 'Life Rafts are Scarce and Small' Dictionary)

The natural boundary

Too many people, already. We get used to living in closed quarters in the cities. The apartments we dwell-in have been shrinking. If you own or lease a flat of 1000 square feet or more you are a privileged person, since the surface is now being sold at around 600 square feet per unit, where you can place a bedroom, a kitchen, a living room, a bathroom and you can fit-in a modular laundry space –Pets not allowed-.

It is by this standpoint a luxury to have a house. No reason to explain what a suburban or country house with a lawn means -"I know", someone explains, "lots of work"-. For sure it is a quite different living standard when, instead of walking to the park, you walk out the door and further to venture into the woods.

"Hey, you all be quiet!" said the ten year old girl to the grownups at the central park picnic. She got everyone's attention.
"Why? What is it?"
"Listen, listen," and as all of them rested attentive. "The sounds of nature." The birds chatting and a squirrel crushing something edible could be heard above the car engines hum.

When was it, that you last listened to your walking over dry leaves and twigs, instead of the stomp-stomp of your feet, over the paved trail going back home? When did you hear something else than the truck's and bus's air-brakes and other people's footsteps, at 5 am in your home town?

The really hard part to understand is how much room a person needs. That of the tiniest of quarters in the belly of a submarine? No windows, no nature scented air, a gray bunk with a table and chair, make up home.

The actual world population density is about 50 people per square kilometer –about a hundred city blocks-, but within city limits we can easily pack 25,000 on the same surface. How many can the planet hold and support comfortably, well fed and happy? The fifty seems to be too many already. Wouldn't you say? Do we need to reach the nose-to-nose limit before we start doing something?

Not a long time back, humanity was thinking along the lines of 'sustained growth' as a healthy population and economic indicator. The name has changed to 'sustained development', which is more realistic, contradictively, the only healthy index truly considered is the market 'growth', not yet seen as an unacceptable concept.
As it was explained before, it is senseless, but still pursued. We have to stop the wagon, slowly let some people off and do not accept new passengers, unless, we'll be brought to throw them out the window, in despair. We need to meet a zero growth rate, meanwhile suffering from anthropophobia.

The limit is not only a social limit, there are resources limits and surface limits. If we get to the space limit it will be too late. It is the time to stop. Let us not fight to death for room or air.

'The space is the limit', you've heard, it isn´t. Our true living quarters are under the thin atmosphere, among trees, oceans, lakes, jungles, deserts and mountains, not inside a rectangular parallelepiped apartment with a low ceiling, awaiting for an earthquake to pulp press us.

Furthermore, we can't successfully have condominiums in space.

Conquering space will not do for our life or economy any good. There are resources that need long hauling, unattainable at most –water and air to begin with-.

The least rooming standard reflects a lot the earthly spaces. The very few experiments of life sustainability, conclude the need for an area of one hectare of green houses to generate oxygen and produce food per four people, along with many technical, operational and social problems that require death-important solutions. Needless to say that failure is breath-taking.

What size will the facilities of the huge Space Station, Moon Apartments or Mars Domes have, for your self-sustained space excursion project? Face it! The best and easiest solution is to stop growing and stay right here on earth, while we solve about the planets for scientific curiosity not as a must because my elbow is already on my neighbor's ribs.

Specific resources and services in specific locations

Fulfilling needs, such as schools, hospitals, entertainment, culture, food, clothing, housing and waste is better controlled when you do not have to make them grow. If people sustain a number, why would you need more schools or hospitals or higher food production? By the time a new hospital is finished you have already been outnumbered. When the main highway is paved the lanes are already insufficient. It seems crazy but the solution is at hand: birth control…against your civil liberties!

People die the natural way, people are born the same natural way, one per one –twins in one case and accidents on the other dispute this-, as simple as that. How do you balance such a thing? The easiest way is –for the greater good- to impede more than two births per couple, although today, to make it more effective, permit only one birth per couple until things stabilize. Your right for a lesser present and future, you may ask...well, on stand-by, for good.

What? What about your markets?
What about them, I answer. Who cares! We are talking about the fate of ourselves and, most of all, the present of ourselves. Why do we have to sacrifice for growth while growth is killing the future? Wake up humanity!
Before killing life, just kill the capital.

Moreover, if we do become regional again, all of our services will also be provided in that way, near-by, within our trusted community, with our traditions and languages. Boring to death, without the daily hustle of our cities, some would say. That may be.

Natural resources are not everywhere, they cannot be forced to go local. Mining will remain as it is. Same goes for all the primary economic activities that are soil or sea bound. We will move materials as needed, not as pleased.

There are more than a couple of goods and services that will need to be generated and delivered through our beloved mass production facilities and network distribution systems, but we should be rational to produce and do the rest outside the scale economy. We need no surplus, no export from the region, except to import what we cannot really produce. Export not to compete, but to trade, to complement, not to amass money that will buy us nothing.
Of course your main energy requirements will come from large power plants, no question. We must be efficient to use the resources available, the space available and the people we count upon. We have to work and coordinate communities in a need-to-do basis. It is not closing doors, building trenches or walls, just moving less merchandise throughout the territories, solving our problems locally.

Why is overpopulation actually a big problem? Because we seem no to see it or not to believe it. Most of the hurdles that countries in the world face, start by having to serve more and more people. People unknowingly grow geometrically, the solutions cannot arrive in the same way, since they grow in linear discrete progressions. Is a mathematical problem that I could plot for you on a Cartesian plane, but would you understand it better? Just don't reproduce, please.

Growing we go, promoting markets, boosting resources consumption and exhaustion. We do not like each other quite enough to live in the same room. Why not make up room for everyone?

THREE- Environmental care

Environment:

"The surroundings" (from the 'Things Defined Simply' Dictionary)

Never trust complexity, even you don't understand it! Why rely on it? (Foreword of the 'Things Defined Simply' Dictionary)

A word on climate change

I truly wouldn't worry too much about climate change. That is not something we can protect, because it is literally out-of-hand.

There are two undisputable data that prove this.
One, that every hundred thousand years -or so-, due to an 'elastic' movement of earth's translation, a cycle begins or ends, where earth undergoes a peak temperature, this –our time- being precisely the warm season, humans present or not.
Two, that the four movements of earth are the major climate shifters.
Of these four movements, one of them causes day and night. There is no question of the temperature changes that involves, the most fortunate result to us being the ability for the planet to cool down on one side, while heating on the other –I am telling you: it's God's make-, causing life to flourish as we know it. We cheat the sun's intentions to roast us.
Another of those movements, along with the tilt of earth, creates the seasons, bringing closer or farther the earth to the sun, on its elliptical movement, again permitting cooling and heating of the hemispheres –God made I´m telling you-.
A third movement we are completely neglecting –really, just as we avoid mentioning the third brother because he did…well, what he did-, called precession –not the third sibling, the movement-, that just causes the enlargement and

shrinkage of the desert zone –did you know the Sahara desert was a jungle and lakes region only 10,000 years ago? Instead of correctly accounting it for the disappearance of some civilizations and the migration to other lands of some others, some say man destroyed it, ha!-. This precession has a cycle of about 26,000 years. So that you get the complete picture of this movement, in 13,000 years the northern hemisphere will have the hottest summer possible, because it will happen on the perihelion, not the aphelion, it will get perpendicular sunlight at the position closer to the sun, not the farthest as it is today. You think nothing happens in 200 years of this swaying rotation? A few degrees of temperature? No? All right, you win, it's not the sun, not the earth's relative position to its radiation, it is human, we, the climate masters!
Finally a nutation movement – the earth nodding at us in disbelief, probably- with a cycle of nine years which I believe corresponds to the rain and draughts cycles we experience over and over again. You see, this last movements rides on top of the wobble, like a tiny vibration, on the precession path.

'The fossil fuels', you may stubbornly insist, 'the carbon dioxide, greenhouse effect'…Keep in mind that data show that the earth has had higher temperatures with lower carbon dioxide levels, so? Tell me, do you believe that the ecosystems have warmed and cooled the earth for thousands of years –in a cycle of course- raising and lowering the carbon dioxide to do so, or that heating and cooling from the distance variation to the sun has produced life and carbon dioxide shifts? In other words, throughout time, has that gas been the cause or the result? The dependent variable, of course. We may influence some at an irrelevant immeasurable amount, please just adapt to the climate heating.

I forgot that we are Gods and that, in our eternal arrogance, we create climate change. Don't be fools, we don't.

It seems that we could for the same reason debate our involvement in the ozone layer hole in the northern pole. You see, the ozone molecule, in order to form, needs UV light. At the angle of radiation impact on the pole there is almost no sunlight coming in, a lot is reflected to space, that's why is cold and why the ozone hole comes to life. However, the observed tendency of depletion or thinning of the layer worldwide was actually reverted after chlorofluorocarbons were banned. Yes we may be Gods.

Again, among the related matters of us being the chosen ones, there is the idea that the trioxygen layer protects life on earth. It may be true, but think about this:

On a summer day, at noon, you lay down on your backyard for a couple of hours dressed with only a bathing suit to enjoy the sun. After that time, you are ready to be transported to a clinic for a nasty sunburn. The grass around you has received the same radiation, no sweat, it is perfect and healthy.

If life on earth had a higher UV influx it would adapt to it! It would be a life needing UV. Some species would go, some others would adjust and remain. The ozone layer is not there to protect us, since we are not the center of creation. Vane, vane, vane, we are. Our climate is there because it is, life evolved as a result to it and it goes as a result of it. Translation, rotation, precession, nutation and the 100,000 year cycle change the life type on earth, create and vanish plants and animals, you know? The same movements facilitate or not the ozone layer formation on the north pole and the melting or freezing of the ice caps –the ice over ground lowering or increasing the average sea level-. We have a different opportunity than the foregone species. We can adapt. Let's do that, based on our acute, precise, predictions of the climate change model, or, is it models?

Yes, of course we can forecast climate change...what? We can't? Then why on earth are we stating and unproven cause for it? If it's not scientifically proven, no known laws explain its behavior, why do you...Oh, I see, 'you think' it is. Don't toss me that bone.

Don´t produce waste

What hasn't been said about the environment? The care for our planet, our house, what haven't we praised? Our for-the-planet awareness is at its peak...yet we trash.

We would be helping our environment, if we produced long lasting things with repairable parts, instead of throw away goods, at best with replaceable parts or, worse, with unfixable possibilities.
We would help if...but it is not the case. We make things that last less and less, basically to indorse productions and markets. Besides our valuable time and effort, this trash-to-be production uses energy and natural resources, emptying the world's warehouses and rapidly affecting the ecosystem by pollution and direct 'tearing apart' of the land, water ways and the sea. Here, we are responsible.

The problem starts there, on the production lines, ending in the disposal of the nearly unused goods we consider obsolete or that no longer function properly or none at all. The new 'technologies' displace them, we trash them. We trash about 1 kg per person per day, 50% of which is organic.

Do we have reusable milk bottles? No, not any more. Do we have reusable anything? No, not at all. Could we have a system like that today? Regional we could, global impossible. Whatever could be reusable or not made with a tiny life span, we are not doing it.
It is as if the producers did not care about what happens to their products when we have no more use for those objects, when they are to be discarded. Their brand ends where it belongs, in a landfill.
But we don't have a determination for the opposite either. We are satisfied with the short use we can make of things, as if infected by the propaganda to renew, to acquire new things, to be in vogue.
We must come to see that we are being robbed, when the products no longer work or can no longer be used, because it

interacted with products and things or systems that have disappeared. Sometimes we face the reality of a product that is not out-of-order but just out-of-time, in perfect shape but useless. What a shame. What a system-made trash.

Corporations must keep their 'client oriented' operations by producing made-to-last goods and repairing the broken ones. We should only buy high quality products, expecting to serve us for a long time.

As for the organic trash, that one that specially interferes with the planet's metabolism, polluting air, water and soil, there is only one thing to say, why are we wasting so much? It is hard to believe that all of it are peelings and bones. I am sure there is also unconsumed food. It is outrageous. Our life of plenty should have its setbacks.

In a very strange way, we believe that all the biodegradable matter is acceptable, inviting us to waste. We are wrong. Just as an example, lixiviates from our organic garbage pollute the soil and all the way down to our water tables. The degradation process of solids takes place both aerobically and anaerobically, generating as pollutants to air: methane, carbon dioxide, hydrogen sulfide, ammonia and some volatile fatty acids, depending on the exact nature of the residue. In concealed bio-digesters things can be controlled and bio gas can be burnt producing water, carbon dioxide and nocuous nitrogen oxides, but using the available energy from the feedstock. When not controlled, the biochemical reactions will take place anyway and release the pollutants.

We cannot avoid garbage, but we can be sensible about it, discarding less.

Restore conditions

Don't destroy in the name of progress. We must find solutions to preserve the environment, but also to preserve what we have built. Usually, when the economic payback period has passed, we are prone to demolish it, to destroy it, to put in the waste basket. The service has already been provided, right?

Nature gets constantly in the way of our wishes. We place the yellow machines at work and redo the landscape according to those desires. The blueprints show us the structure and face of the project, affecting more than just the plowed area. The surroundings receive, during the project and afterwards, the impact of the new activity the project implicates.

Sometimes projects evolve into other ones, reshaping the place over and over. But there comes the time when the projects are abandoned forever. Restoring the environment has not been one of our goals.

When it comes to industrial projects, we may pollute that lagoon or creek, simply raising the water temperature by a few degrees, changing its acidity or alkalinity, reducing the oxygen dissolved or increasing its salinity. Every change modifies the ecosystems. It adapts or dies. Of course it is not economically wise to avoid that impact. It never is.
It is in our interest, as the people that live near that place, to reduce all affectations and to restore its original conditions. Is it?

Nature, someone told us, exists for our personal use and take, somebody says it's sacred, yet another said it's a survival need to preserve it. Take your pick, but be responsible about the consequences. You are accountable today.

CONCLUSION

CONCLUSION

The final judgment

Conclusion has, as many words, several meanings, one of them being just the end of something. This is that case. However I may try to summon ideas and compressed them into a meaningful final judgment –not that 'final judgment'-.

Our way of life, whether we see it or not, accepted or disliked, is structured to the convenience of the rulers of our society, as it has always been -pharaonic as it may sound-. How bad is it? Your answer depends on how you have been favored within the system. That is the real problem, it doesn't favor all. There are the citizens and the *pariah*.

The system's life is filled with lies and dogmatic concepts that we take as they come. Elegant, but disrobed of meanings, like democracy, justice, freedom or equality. Something is wrong, we feel it, endure it. Once in a while we disagree, but we mostly comply. Such is life!
Of course some others think that everything is all right. The problems undergone by the people are due to their own attitude.

The system, really, can only be as strong as its population. Wouldn't you say? However, the population that has to be considered today is that of the whole globe, since we are, for practical purposes, about to cover it all. Globalization has reached us finally, for worse.

The system should be, economic, political and socially feasible for all -It is not today by far-. It needs to be harmonically integrated, respecting peoples and cultures, otherwise it will continue to fail -because it is failing, don't doubt it-. Capital, by imposing a wealth gap and legalizing abuse, is destroying human diversity -the planet itself, as well- and creating great social discomfort.

We have to benefit from the oncoming scientific developments, but if humanity does not come to a reasonable life understanding, with a decent justice for all, we will use science to our disadvantage and eventual annihilation –may it happen if we don't prove to deserve otherwise-.

The real hurdles for the future are moral and social, but there are a couple entirely technical: the lack of power to transport and an excess population. We may adapt to nature's changes and catastrophes, but I am not so sure about our own nature.

The strong foundations of our civilization are actually brittle...and crumbling. Get out of the building now! Before it collapses.

The distorted image

One day, maybe closer than we expect, a space traveler will reach our planet on a clear skies night. The first image, while making its approach, will be a fascinating surface of scattered lights. Perhaps, guided by curiosity, the galactonaut will steer the vessel towards a thicker glowing spot. Upon reaching one of our major cities, the shiny glass walled buildings, the geometrical streets, the moving vehicles will spike the scientist, leading our galactonaut to land. The next morning, while carefully disguised and mingling with the crowd, the image will be distorted. The real civilization with all its social flaws will come disappointedly into view. After studying our behavioral codes and matching it to our doings, the written report back home will read at the conclusion, 'Scientifically advanced but socially primitive, useless to contact'

Table of Contents

Foreword   5
Part I: Foundations   9
        One- Snob   11
        Two- The hive   17
        Three- The fourth power – Freedom   22
        Four- Democracy   28
        Five- Justice   40
        Six- Égalité   45
        Seven- Productivity   58
        Eight- Competitiveness and the free market   67
        Nine- GDP/GNP and macro /micro Indicators   75
        Ten- Inflation, that relentless ghost   85
        Eleven- The financial system   91
        Twelve- Taxes and the government   103
        Thirteen- Surveillance   111
        Fourteen- Health   115
        Fifteen- The greedy society   121
        Sixteen- The capital   126
Epilogue to the foundations   151
Part II: Shockwaves   153
        One- Arrogance   155
        Two- The greater good   159
        Three- The other civilizations   165
        Four- The world's ~~bureaucracy~~ management   174
        Five- Advanced science   181
        Six- War   193
Part III: A defying future   195
        One- Energy   200
        Two- Overpopulation   210
        Three- Environmental care   215
Conclusion   221

28862649R00138

Made in the USA
Columbia, SC
28 October 2018